SACRAMENTO PUBLIC LIBRARY

Foundation

THIS BOOK WAS DONATED BY

The Sacramento Public Library Foundation
Books and Materials Endowment

The Sacramento Public Library gratefully acknowledges this
contribution to support and improve Library services in the community.

sac
spb SACRAMENTO PUBLIC LIBRARY

THE
PIRATE
ORGANIZATION

Lessons from the
Fringes of Capitalism

RODOLPHE DURAND

JEAN-PHILIPPE VERGNE

HARVARD BUSINESS REVIEW PRESS

Boston, Massachusetts

No part of this publication may be reproduced, stored in, or introduced into a retrieval system, or transmitted, in any form, or by any means (electronic, mechanical, photocopying, recording, or otherwise), without the prior permission of the publisher. Requests for permission should be directed to permissions@hbsp.harvard.edu, or mailed to Permissions, Harvard Business School Publishing, 60 Harvard Way, Boston, Massachusetts 02163.

The web addresses referenced in this book were live and correct at the time of the book's publication but may be subject to change.

First published in French as *L'Organisation Pirate: Essai sur l'évolution du capitalisme*

Mondes Marchands Collections, directed by Benoît Heilbrunn

© Éditions LE BORD DE L'EAU 2010

www.editionsbdl.com

33310 Lormont, France

ISBN: 978-2-35687-084-1

Library of Congress Cataloging-in-Publication Data

Durand, Rodolphe.

[Organisation pirate. English]

The pirate organization : lessons from the fringes of capitalism / Rodolphe Durand and Jean-Philippe Vergne.

    p. cm.

"First published in French as L'Organisation Pirate: Essai sur l'évolution du capitalisme."

ISBN 978-1-4221-8318-2 (alk. paper)

1. Pirates. 2. Computer hackers. 3. Hacktivism. 4. Capitalism—History—21st century. I. Vergne, Jean-Philippe. II. Title.

G535.D8813 2012

364.16'4—dc23

2012025303

The paper used in this publication meets the requirements of the American National Standard for Permanence of Paper for Publications and Documents in Libraries and Archives Z39.48-1992.

To our readers

CONTENTS

Preface   ix

Acknowledgments   xi

1. Introduction   1

2. What Is Piracy?   9

3. The Pirate Organization and Territorial
   Expansion, or Why Capitalists
   Shouldn't Hate the State   17

4. Pirate or Corsair?   29

5. What Is the Pirate Organization?   41

6. Where It All Began: The Pirate Organization
   on the High Seas   59

7. Why Piracy Is Not Just About Economics   71

8. The Pirate Organization on the Airwaves   81

9. The Pirate Organization and the Monopolist   87

10. The Pirate Organization in Cyberspace   101

11. Hacking Property Rights   111

12. Is the Pirate Organization a Fair Competitor?   123

13. The Pirate Organization and the Building
Blocks of Life   133

14. The Future of the Capitalist State   145

15. Conclusion: To the Fringes and Back   153

Notes   165

Bibliography   173

Index   179

About the Authors   193

PREFACE

The Pirate Organization is not just a book but a broad interdisciplinary project aimed at connecting the social sciences, contemporary artistic creation, and civil society. This book was first published in French in 2010, accompanied by the release of an original musical composition by the experimental rock band Chevreuil. The production of the music was funded from the authors' royalties, and the composition was published under a Creative Commons license to allow for a broad diffusion. Tracks for each instrument were and still are available for download separately to facilitate the remixing—or hacking—of the song.

This extended and updated version of the book, published in English for the first time, is accompanied by a short animation movie directed by Daniel Wyatt and titled *What Is the Pirate Organization?* It is also published under a Creative Commons license, and the movie's soundtrack uses fragments from Chevreuil's original music as well as excerpts from remixes of the song sent to us by our readers.

This new version of *The Pirate Organization* incorporates many of the suggestions we were lucky enough to receive from colleagues, friends, and readers. We are always happy to discuss and receive feedback to refine or expand our ideas, so e-mails and tweets (*@PirateOrg*) are always welcome. Links to the music and movie can be found at http://twitter.com/PirateOrg. Enjoy.

ACKNOWLEDGMENTS

Chevreuil: Tony C. and Julien F.

Eve Chiapello

Annie L. Cot

Thomas Gayno

Benoit Heilbrunn

Thomas Heller

Gregory Jost

Xavier Labatie

PointB Worklodge: Karin and Mark and Margarita
(pointb.org)

Clara Seidl

Social Sciences and Humanities Research Council of
Canada

Society and Organizations
(www.societyandorganizations.org)

Tim Sullivan and the whole team at Harvard Business
Review Press

Floor van den Born

Jean-Charles Vergne

Jean-Luc Veyssy

Jérôme Vidal

Daniel Wyatt

The authors also want to thank their colleagues at
HEC Paris, New York University (Stern), and Western
University (Ivey) for their friendly support. Many other
people made this book possible; they know who they are.

THE
PIRATE
ORGANIZATION

INT𝒬ODUCTION

It would be a tremendous story if the author of the mythical text about the rise of capitalism was also the author of a history of pirates. However, this is not simple coincidence.

—Toshiya Ueno, "Piracy Now and Then"[1]

Pirates appear at pivotal periods in history. When capitalism began to spread along the trading routes toward the Indies. When radio opened an era of mass communication. When the Internet became part of the global economy. When the biotech revolution began bubbling to the surface. And it's no coincidence that these four Golden Ages of piracy correspond to major turning points in the history of capitalism. In fact, we argue, piracy could very well be one of the drivers of capitalism's growth and evolution. Piracy is not random. It is predictable. And it cannot be separated from capitalism.

Many think of piracy as a mere blot on the vast backdrop of history, a subject that deserves only a passing mention

in serious studies. In sea tales pirates appear as seafaring heroes, but in our history books they are characters with minor roles.[2] Yet pirates are etched in the collective memory of different places and eras: buccaneers and radio DJs on the sea, cyberpirates on the web and biopirates in the lab, tinkering with DNA, the heart of living organisms.

We use the word *pirate* to describe such a wide range of actors. But there exists a much deeper relationship between these various forms of piracy. We believe that a shared series of traits, roles, and tactics brings together pirates of all stripes into an organized form we call the *pirate organization*.

Our research has revealed a number of essential traits shared by all pirates. First, pirates are not solitary heroes who challenge authority out of fury or despair. Rather, they organize themselves into groups, which in some cases grow to several thousand strong. These groups are built to reach specific goals, forge alliances, negotiate with enemies, and engage in conflict—thus our focus on the pirate organization.

Like piracy, the scope and nature of capitalism are hard to define. Capitalism is the bedrock of our society, yet it seems to contain the seeds of its own destruction. In political discussions, capitalism proves an easy target because it provides a simple cause for some of our most complex problems. What lurks behind global warming? Capitalism. What triggered the stock market crisis? Capitalism. China's meteoric growth? The price of paintings at the last Sotheby's auction? The decline of religion and the bland taste of supermarket tomatoes?

It is easy to find loud activists who either hate or love capitalism. Capitalism as a theory has seeped into our public consciousness, but it has become increasingly difficult to agree on the breadth of the term itself and on its dynamics. It is therefore neither by accident nor out of sheer provocation that we wish to explore both piracy *and* capitalism. We believe that capitalism is in part based on the give-and-take relationship between the pirate organization and the sovereign state, which came about at precisely the same period when capitalism was born. By sketching a theory of the pirate organization, we hope this work serves also as a modest essay on the evolution of capitalism, viewed from its fringes.

Many talented historians have developed unquestionable expertise in maritime piracy. In the near future, a new generation of academics will write the history of cyberpiracy and biopiracy. But given the specialization that is required to study such complex topics, it is unlikely that historians will one day develop a cross-disciplined analysis of all types of piracy. Besides, this is not their role. Economists tend to break down capitalism into a group of variables and indicators that must be arranged and adjusted in order for society to reach its full harmonious potential. Needless to say, piracy is not part of the equation—at best it is seen as a discordant ring of negative externalities that must be quelled. And sociologists tend to impose artificial limits on themselves by looking at society through the prism of social class and yet fail to capture the role of the pirate organizations in both market and nonmarket situations.

Societal and economic phenomena cannot be reduced to disciplinary quirks. Therefore, we are taking on this venture as students of organizations in an effort to sway the discussion from individuals and markets. Individuals, despite their intimate desires, cannot reform the structure of economic and social exchanges. Without organizations and coordinated resources, they are powerless. And we have grown tired of newspaper headlines such as "What Do Markets Want from the Fed?" Markets do not want anything. Why? Because markets, as abstract aggregates, are not purposeful, whereas bank X or hedge fund Y is. And those happen to be organizations. And unlike individuals, they have enough power to influence the course of history. Our primary level of analysis, therefore, will be organizations (especially pirate organizations). We have high hopes that this interdisciplinary, organization-level approach will pique interest and spark a debate on contemporary phenomena, including those that go beyond piracy.

In the remainder of the book, the reader will find detailed accounts of how pirates operate to shape the contours of capitalism across history. This book can be seen as a journey across time and space. It can be read as a short history of piracy or alternatively as a short history of capitalism. Each chapter finds its background in a different place at a particular time in history. The journey will begin in chapter 2 in ancient Rome, where sea banditry came to be known as piracy for the first time. Yet we will later argue in chapter 3 that the true meaning of piracy only unfolds in the aftermath of Christopher Columbus's

discovery of the Americas, as the notions of territory, sovereign state, and capitalism acquire their modern definition. That's why in chapter 4 we will spend some time with the sea pirates of the sixteenth and seventeenth centuries, who for the first time in history explicitly contest the legal tools by which sovereign states impose norms upon conquered territories—in this case, the high seas. Importantly, we will distinguish between pirates and corsairs and explain why this distinction is useful to understand the history of capitalism from an organizational perspective.

Chapter 5 will give the reader a flavor of the bigger picture—that is, of how different forms of piracy (on the seas, on the airwaves, in cyberspace, or at the heart of DNA) relate to each other and keep telling us a very consistent story on the nature of capitalism. After we have justified our perspective about the need to study piracy as consistently organized action rather than as a series of heroic individual achievements, chapter 6 will go back in time to investigate the roots of sea pirates' activism against the state's self-granted monopoly on economic and social norms definition. Pirate organizations, across time and space, have often taken a stance against the state to defend what we term a *public cause*. So in chapter 7 we bolster our claim that an interdisciplinary approach to piracy is required to avoid the damaging reductionism of a purely economic examination of the phenomenon, which intends to rationalize everything based on the holy trinity of cost-risk-benefit analysis.

Chapter 8 makes a jump in time and space to the early-twentieth-century United Kingdom, where pirate radio stations started waging a war against the state-sponsored monopoly of the British Broadcasting Corporation (BBC). As we will see, the pirates played a key role in defining the norms of radio broadcasting that most of us have known between the mid-1960s and the beginning of the twenty-first century. Chapter 9 reflects upon this struggle and outlines a few reasons why the pirate organization, no matter where and when, usually engages in an outright struggle against different forms of monopolistic organization. In that chapter, we also draw an essential distinction between capitalism and free markets as we are forced to recognize, based on our review of modern history, that capitalism always expands into new territories using monopolies as conveyor belts, such as the East India Companies on the high seas or the BBC on the airwaves. This, we believe, has tremendous political implications that many loud activists of today should keep in mind as they blame, helter-skelter, both free markets *and* big-business capitalism for all the evils in the world.

Chapter 10 will get us closer to the present time by deciphering the inner workings of pirate organizations in cyberspace. Recent events, such as the repeated assaults of WikiLeaks against various corporations and governments or Obama's buildup of cyberwar capabilities, will help us illustrate vividly how mythical tales of sea piracy are likely to travel from the high seas into cyberspace in the coming years. But one should not feel uncomfortable because

of the ghostliness of the twenty-first-century cyberpirates. In fact, we will maintain that they are not that different from the seventeenth-century sea pirates. Chapter 11 gives some important background information on our system of intellectual property rights and, without going into the technicalities, draws the portrait of a new type of pirate organization called *troll*, which thrives on exploiting the system's internal contradictions. This leads us to discuss, in chapter 12, how pirate organizations manage to compete with what we call the legitimate *organizations of the milieu*, which operate with the benediction and support of the state. True, the survival chances of pirate organizations are pretty low compared with those of large listed corporations—but despite a shorter life expectancy, pirates manage to profoundly alter our societies. More precisely, pirate organizations are communities where alternative norms of social interaction and economic exchange are designed, before they start diffusing throughout the broader social fabric.

Chapter 13 takes us a step further by looking at biopiracy, whose ultimate consequences could entail the redefinition of life forms at a deeper, biogenetic level—together with the granting of the right to make a profit out of it. Biopiracy is still nascent, but it will certainly be one of the biggest challenges of the twenty-first century, affecting many industries, such as agriculture and biotech, but also mankind as a whole. In chapter 14, we take a step back and critically assess the current sovereign state system's ability to deal with the increasing power and legitimacy

that reside with pirate organizations, especially those operating in cyberspace and manipulating DNA. Put simply, we speculate about the end of a world that was born in 1492 and became adult in 1648 with the Treaty of Westphalia—a world guided by the now ailing nation-state system for the last four centuries. How much longer can it last? In the future, which organizations will be best positioned to legitimize economic exchanges in territories such as cyberspace? Nation-states, organizations of the milieu, or pirate organizations? Chapter 15, the conclusion, wraps up the argument and suggests paying more attention to the lessons we can learn from the fringes of capitalism. The last pages also set the stage for an *orgology of capitalism*—namely, an interdisciplinary study of capitalism from the viewpoint of the organizations that wrote its history, and will continue to do so in the future.

WHAT IS PIRACY?

Piracy may be a blot on civilization and its practitioners criminals whom it is a duty to extirpate. Yet there will always be a sympathetic response in the human heart to the appeal of the adventurer who dares go to far and dangerous places and in defiance of all organized respectability take his courage in both hands to carve out his fortune.

—Philip Gosse, *History of Pirates*

The word *pirate* comes from the ancient Greek word *peirao*, which means "to put to the test." Analysis of ancient texts reveals that *pirate* had a broader application beyond a few notorious rebels who gained fame through their crimes. Entire villages, even small societies, were considered piratical if they refused to submit to local authorities. If they did refuse, Greek city-states or Roman towns would use force to persuade them. Piracy, in this form, occurred in many different places. Pirates acted on both land and sea. They occupied small patches of land, or they spread out

across the country, in small or large groups. But they had one thing in common: they crossed all established limits of order.[1]

Piracy in Ancient Times

Although Cicero declared pirates to be the "common enemies of all man" (*communis hostis omnium*), they weren't local criminals or intruders from far-off lands. The foundations of piracy are the result of many factors. All towns and cities, as they do today, had norms, laws, and trade practices. Pirates broke away from these. What makes a pirate is what he sets his sights on, what he seeks to change, what he proposes as an opponent of a particular society. Pirates obeyed neither the laws of the land nor any other identifiable law. As a result, one could not negotiate with them. You couldn't trust them. To even talk to a pirate was a fundamental violation of the law. The pirate could corrupt law-abiding citizens by opening their eyes to a parallel world where the concept of territory and property did not exist. For Cicero, like many of his successors, doing business with a pirate was to venture to the other side of the mirror.

By their actions, pirates sent both a criminal and a political message to the societies they were fighting against. They were not mere bandits, per se, so they did not fall under the orders and scales of legal justice. They fell between the cracks of law. To the state, they were not clear enemies,

because they did not fly a national flag and they lacked
an established government. The pirate eluded the friend/
enemy dichotomy put forth by judges and legal scholars
since, according to the law, piracy fell outside the realm of
political influence. The pirate was considered "denational-
ized": with pirates, neither war nor peace was possible.

Moreover, the Roman concept of piracy laid the foundation for legal property. The pirate steals something, or
he appropriates the right to it. But we shouldn't make the
mistake of reducing piracy to a question of illegal property,
since pirates also rejected the legitimacy of the "prize law"
that the Romans had worked so hard to establish. This
sulan, or law of reprisals, enabled the Roman legion to use
violence to recoup damages. If the pirate was not the enemy
of the people, he was at least the enemy of political and
legal power, since he rejected the concept of "legitimate
ownership" and efforts to compensate for damages without
declaring war. Pirates did not declare conflicts or recognize the damages they inflicted on a city-state or empire.
They used force without legal authority, unlike the political powers that confronted them.

Historians have long been interested in the characteristics that bring together and set apart kingdoms and
pirates. Take Pompey, who in 67–66 BC negotiated with
several bands of pirates to get them to settle down, to stop
hindering commercial development. Ironically, the pirate
and the emperor share a common characteristic: they both
use power to appropriate and rule. The response of a con-
victed pirate to Alexander the Great, as reported by Saint

Augustine in *De Civitate Dei*, is enlightening: "Because I only have one rickety ship, I'm called a bandit, and because you have a large fleet, you are called an emperor." Saint Augustine then added a key nuance: "Without justice, in fact, are kingdoms nothing more than a large band of thieves? And what is a band of thieves if not a small kingdom? Because it is a gathering of men with a leader, in which a social covenant is recognized, and which has certain conventions governing the sharing of the spoils." However, without sufficient power to allow them to go from unspeakable to unpunished, deprived of the attributes establishing legitimacy and justice, the pirates lack legal influence over their earthly possessions.

So here's the twist: while depriving others of their goods and rights, pirates cannot claim to own anything. This is a considerable difference that sets them apart from kings and emperors.

The Eternal Return of Piracy

Piracy has experienced a few Golden Ages. The classical era Mediterranean abounds with accounts of high-seas bandits attacking Greek and Roman city-states. Until the nineteenth century, the Mediterranean continued to experience many acts of piracy, and pirates settled in major ports on the Moroccan (Salé) and Algerian (Algiers, Tangiers) coasts. In popular stories the Caribbean is often the epicenter of piracy. Buccaneers from the eighteenth century, who were former

European infantry and marines sailing the Caribbean seas, set up camps on Tortoise Island and Santo Domingo, from which they would launch attacks. Together, they boarded Spanish and Portuguese vessels, flushing the sailors from their hideouts. A few decades later, the English allowed the pirates to start a settlement in Jamaica in order to mount a defense against a Spanish attempt to reconquer the islands.

In the United States, the last captain sentenced for piracy, Nathaniel Gordon, was executed in 1862, amid multiple protests, for a crime that sank into oblivion. Since then, piracy has had periods of growth and decline. Given the increased security deployed by coast guards, customs officers, and national naval forces, some predicted piracy's extinction on the seas. Others see piracy as an adaptable phenomenon: pirates resemble counterfeiters, who embrace the most recent technological developments to produce increasingly realistic fakes. Like counterfeiters, today's pirates reputedly adopt the most state-of-the-art means to cause states and firms the same problems as the sea rovers did, centuries ago.

Currently, there's a surge of high-seas piracy, especially in the Gulf of Aden, located between Somalia and Yemen. The International Maritime Organization annually recorded fifty incidents of piracy in the mid-1980s, two hundred fifty a decade later, and more than five hundred in the mid-2000s. In 2006, fifteen crew members were killed and approximately two hundred were taken hostage. But are today's Somali pirates akin to seventeenth-century free-booters? Tentatively, our answer is no. High-seas banditry

is not tantamount to the type of organized piracy that seeks to reshuffle how capitalist economies work.

So who are the real contemporary pirates? The airwaves have their pirate radio stations; the web has its cyberpirates; and DNA, at the heart of living species, has become the locus of interest for biopirates. Governments and companies across the world take these new forms of piracy very seriously, and with good reason. In June 2011, a report published by the Organization for Economic Cooperation and Development (OECD) evaluated cyberpiracy as one of the five biggest threats to the global economy. In the last few months, several cyberattacks made news: pirates from Anonymous looted Sony's online gaming databases, Lulz Security broke into CIA servers, and unidentified attackers stole Citigroup's confidential customer data, to name a few.

But what is the common thread among these pirate phenomena? We have decided to not put everyone in the same basket. In fact, this decision was the main motive behind the writing of this book. Committing an illegal act at sea does not make one a pirate—if so, fishing for tuna off season would be an act of piracy, as would smoking pot on a yacht. Nor is it enough to steal something by force—otherwise, bank robbers would be considered pirates, too.

We maintain that the growth of capitalism into new, technology-driven areas (oceans, airwaves, the net, DNA) goes hand in hand with the emergence of new forms of piracy. Therefore, our theory of piracy shows that pirates, regardless of the time period, share the following features: they enter into a conflictive "relationship" with the

state, especially when the state claims to be the sole source of sovereignty; they operate in an organized manner on uncharted territory, from a set of support bases located outside this territory, over which the state typically claims sovereign control; they develop, as alternative communities, a series of discordant norms that, according to them, should be used to regulate uncharted territory; and ultimately, they represent a threat to the state because they upset the very ideas of sovereignty and territory by contesting the state's control and the activities of the legal entities that operate under its jurisdiction, such as for-profit corporations and monopolies.

As these points develop, we will reveal the bigger picture: with the birth of modern capitalism, the pirate organization gained power as a transhistorical force. And as we develop our theory of the pirate organization, we will also hint at a theory of capitalism. And that is why Blackbeard, for example, has far more in common with a cyberpirate than with a Somalian peasant who uses a Kalashnikov to attack a fishing boat from a makeshift craft.

THE PIRATE ORGANIZATION AND TERRITORIAL EXPANSION

or

Why Capitalists Shouldn't Hate the State

The specifically legal concept of "territory" is a creation of modern times … Government officials have used new triangulation, topographical and mapping technologies to precisely determine the space covered by national jurisdiction. This process started coming into play in the 17th century.

—Heller-Roazen, *The Enemy of All*

To understand the pirate organization, we have to clarify exactly what kind of waters it operates in. That is, we must clarify what we mean by *capitalism*, given the persistent myth that likens it to a form of hyperindividualism.

Capitalism must be set apart from the series of abstract principles used to lay the foundations of neoclassical economic theory, which studies the ultimate consequences of a state of the world in which the trading of any merchandise is carried out within a system entirely determined by the free fluctuation of price based on supply and demand. These free, pure, and perfect competitive conditions do not exist anywhere and have never existed: they describe an abstract framework that fuels the theoretical development of a scientific discipline.

Most critics of economics nevertheless continue to consider that the discipline can be reduced to *neoclassical* economics (which is wrong) or that economists are just a group of idealists who would truly want the real world to mirror their theory, which, with few exceptions, is also incorrect. Yet it is true that many economists hold their share of responsibility in the unfortunate association of capitalism with neoclassical theory that they have for some time helped disseminate.

Our view of history places the emergence of capitalism at the time when a twofold deterritorialization and normalization movement became effective. By *deterritorialization*, we mean the process whereby capital, workforce, or resources are ripped off of a given territory and become largely independent from it. And what we term *normalization* is the process by which norms, in the broad sense, are imposed upon a space and turn it into a territory. These two principles, which we will explicate further in the next few pages, are the distinctive features of capitalistic dynam-

ics. Symbolically, the birth of modern capitalism began in 1492 with the discovery of America, and it ended in 1648 with the Treaty of Westphalia, which ratified the terms and conditions under which a modern sovereign state could operate.[1]

Sovereignty of State and Capitalism

In line with the spirit of this treaty, the key political event of the seventeenth century was the acquisition of sovereignty by the European states. The sovereignty of the state is the process by which all the land under royal influence becomes territory. As a direct property of the monarch, territory implies the normalization of land without feudal mediation: any individual living in the territory goes from being a subject of a vassal, who serves the king to the nth degree, to the direct subject of the sovereign. Clusters of fiefs then mold into one sovereign territory, emancipating from the church, from the nobility, and from merchant city-states.[2] Consequently, an expansion of territory is primarily an expansion of sovereignty—the homogeneous texture that facilitates the flow of merchandise, money, soldiers, taxes, and labor.

The economic development that took place in sixteenth- and seventeenth-century Europe is inseparable from the institutions that accompanied the birth of the modern sovereign state. The emergence of sovereign European states is the circumstance behind the upcoming upheav-

als in the organization of international trade. Modern economic changes could not have taken place without the institutional proliferation that secured property rights, such as those that oversaw the advent of the process of enclosure. This proliferation is orchestrated by the sovereign state, which has carte blanche to develop the legal, fiscal, and military tools required for its own reproduction and expansion.

Capitalism, therefore, as a sufficiently homogeneous social formation anchored in identified territories, allows for the circulation and combination of labor and capital. This combination did not take place during feudal times, because peasants were too land rooted. Capital stocks were almost nonexistent, and the local markets, divided up by local micropowers, were too rough and segmented. The serf is a product of the land that he cultivates, and the land is but a facade under which capital lurks. In a feudal society, labor and capital are simply appendages of the land.

Capitalism came into play when "land" became "territory," when the link between labor and capital loosened, and when the sovereign states began to implement norms for economic circulation and exchange. If the Middle Ages were the age of land, capitalism is the age of territory. The sovereign state, by imposing a set of norms on its territory, enables the deterritorialization of labor and capital. By limiting the power of city-states, which had the habit of imposing taxes and the rules of local guilds on traveling merchants, the sovereign state increased the possibilities of

circulation and sped up the flow of capital and labor—and this was going to change the course of history.

Capitalism and Deterritorialization

The concept of *capitalism* came into use during the second half of the nineteenth century, and, retrospectively, stood for the emergence of a social form that saw trade in a radically different way from what prevailed in feudal societies.[3] Capitalism, according to some, is a social order that allows organizational forms to combine flows (of labor and capital) and process them according to particular rules of exchange. Capitalism enables the exchange and combination of mobile resources across definite territories on which sovereigns, be they queens, parliaments, or courts, guarantee the enforcement of norms (e.g., rules and laws). Capitalism, therefore, fosters the gathering of productive resources without territories ("deterritorialized") by capital owners who invest in their localized combination and future value. On new territories, too, capitalist entrepreneurs combine deterritorialized resources: for instance, labor that migrates to a novel settlement, raw materials transported to a production site where specially designed machines have been installed, and economic institutions like written contracts or business law that can be reproduced over time and space.

This deterritorialization of resources leads to the collapse of feudal codes: the peasant can no longer be attached to his

parish; the serf can no longer depend on the local lordship. To integrate these resources into legitimate production, the state decrees standards for trade and the appropriation of any surplus. Thus, two dialectic movements are at the basis of the rise in power of capitalism: on the one hand, the deterritorialization of capital, resources, and labor, and their reterritorialization into the trade space; on the other hand, the normalization of this trade space through the definition and enforcement of norms that delineate legitimate exchanges.

The flight of the Huguenots, the brain drain, and the gold rush are famous examples of deterritorialization. A contemporary example of reterritorialization is the relocation of Native Americans to protected reserves and to tax-free areas where they can develop gambling-based businesses. The legitimization of any form of economic exchange (bartering, below-cost pricing, credit purchasing), of trade (sale of alcohol, slaves, or firearms), or of competition (monopoly, regulated oligopoly, free trade) constitutes a normalization process orchestrated by the state, which, for several centuries, has been carving out the possible trajectories of capitalism. From this perspective, free trade is no more "natural" than monopoly. It is the visible hand of the state that contributes to shaping the early competitive structure of most industries in any capitalist society.

The deterritorialization of men, resources, and goods was facilitated by a series of events that occurred simultaneously on both land and sea. In the sixteenth century,

the rise in enclosure gave birth in Great Britain to modern farms, which were managed by large landowners, who focused on productivity and profit gains. Subsistence farming was being gradually replaced by intensive agriculture, which allowed landowners to accumulate wealth while forcing thousands of impoverished peasants to seek labor in city factories, whose emergence was made possible by the growing availability of investment capital. At the same time, improved navigation techniques created a potential for deterritorialization toward new continents. European sovereigns thus had new areas to exploit precious metals and labor power, which began to spread worldwide. The emergence of an international banking system, the widespread use of substitutes for coinage (bill of exchange, currency), and the normalization of risk by insurance companies has sped up this worldwide movement of deterritorialization. This set the stage for a redefinition of statehood.

Normalization of Exchanges

The notion of sovereignty has taken different meanings over time. In primitive societies, the sovereign was the one who claimed control over the forces of nature. Kings and shamans could equally refer to the sun as the source of their legitimate power. Throughout the Middle Ages, in despotic societies, the supreme leader found his legitimacy in the size of his land possessions—and sovereignty,

literally, was rooted in the land controlled by lords and emperors.

In the modern age, it is capital (or money) that fills this function. Each and every thing can be converted to a value that is scaled against a currency that ensures perfect comparability across the many forms that capital can take on. Not anchored anymore in land possessions, cut and split up multiple times, deterritorialized resources can flow and be combined more freely under the ruling and protection of sovereign states, which enforce a homogeneous set of rules in a given territory. These rules determine once and again how to trade and exchange novel productions. Their deployment and subsequent enforcement form the core of the normalization process, which is essential for capitalism's expansion. Sovereign states had to take important measures to remove the preexisting binds that tied capital to land, such as imposing a single unit of measure for weighing goods or enforcing the use of a single language across merchant cities (e.g., when the meter was first defined in eighteenth-century France, more than seven hundred different units of measure were in use).

To prosper, societies require order. Before the modern age, order was often controlled by a lone despot, whose desire for power was mediated by the social machinery of the city, the empire, or the fief. With the advent of the modern state, the normative apparatus or "code" deployed by sovereigns has considerably expanded, and it now trickles downward to citizens. This code superimposes itself upon society. Norms affect many aspects of life—social,

economic, political, and religious. Some people denounce sovereigns, mainly for their capacity to "overcode" the lives of their citizens. We speak of "overcoding" to make it clear that sovereigns always superimpose their norms over a code that was already there and in use before they came to power. Sovereignty does not emerge spontaneously and typically has to wipe out previously existing social rules to achieve dominance. The nonconformists who disagree—the philosophers, artists, entrepreneurs, activists, or bankers— either alone or en masse, decode, make explicit, and rewrite the principles that give meaning to social and productive activities. In return, the sovereign has to justify his own code, prohibit new norms, and fight against those who try to reveal the downsides of overcoding, its totalitarianism and its fundamental, soul-sucking nature. The state is blinded by its own norms and its fear of losing control over the outcomes of economic exchanges.

Capitalists succeed by constantly reshaping the conditions of the pursuit of their own goals. A capitalistic crisis is nothing but a burst of energy that destroys old norms and gives birth to a new way of working: the tulip crisis (or tulip bubble) in the 1630s was a warning against the first exotic-speculative instruments of the Amsterdam Stock Market. The stock market crash of 1929 brought attention to the risk posed by the general authorization of credit share purchasing. The financial crises of 2008 and 2011 showed the limits of the securitization of private and public debts. If there is one thing that will not kill capitalism, it is a capitalistic crisis, which systematically outsmarts

all the talking heads predicting its demise and all analysts
who infer from their research the death of the system. Since
the very beginning, it has been part of capitalism's nature to
keep redefining its own rules, each time pushing its limits
further. Through the burst of crises, new codes emerge that
are reintegrated into the capitalist logic.

The seventeenth century was a time of such normalization on the seas. European sovereigns established new
trade territories in which the deterritorialized flows of
labor and capital could circulate, opening capitalism up to
new ways of exchanging, thinking, working, and resist-
ing. The period saw the normalizing of codes of acceptable practices in the new territory: defining which legal
entities are allowed to trade within legitimate territories,
establishing which measures must be used to account for
and record economic activity, and determining the conditions under which products and goods can be sold. The
United Provinces, for instance, simultaneously saw the
appearance in the seventeenth century of the East India
Company, which produced, shipped, and traded spices
and luxury goods; of the letter of marque and reprisal,
which controlled the activity of merchants in Southeast
Asia; and of the spice market of Amsterdam, which structured the consumption of goods at home by making their
relative price known to consumers. All of these are institutional innovations promoted by the state to enforce new
norms that would define the contours of capitalism for
the next couple of centuries.

Capitalism, the State, and the Invisible Hand of Classical Liberalism

Capitalism is not liberalism. Liberalism refers to a philosophical movement and the political system that derived from it.[4] Originally, eighteenth-century liberalists defended individual freedom against the absolutism of European sovereigns—the very ones who laid the stones of capitalism.[5] Free trade is one of several possible transpositions of liberal thought onto the market sphere, but we should not see any necessity in the cohabitation of liberalist economics and capitalism. Free market economics promotes individual interest and market allocation as the two pillars of production, exchange, and wealth creation, a movement that has gained momentum since the 1980s. However, the first two centuries of European capitalism or its recent transfiguration in post-Communist China serve as two glaring examples of nonliberalist capitalistic societies. Conversely, models of noncapitalistic liberalism exist in most government-free societies or utopias, be they seventeenth-century pirates of yore or Vietnam-era hippies.

Coincidentally, it is while living in these antiestablishment, peace-and-love communities in the early 1970s that the first cyberpirates honed their craft. Within technophile circles, activists such as Abbie Hoffman or John Perry Barlow organized movements to gain technical prowess through hacking in an effort to free new digital spaces from state-controlled normalization. And John Perry Barlow,

the former lyricist for the Grateful Dead, later became the author of "A Declaration of the Independence of Cyberspace." Capitalism and liberalism are not synonymous, and neither are anticapitalism and antiliberalism.

Capitalism and the sovereign state are consubstantially linked, not opposed. The idea of capitalism without government is a quasi-perfect oxymoron, and so is the anarcho-capitalist pipe dream of a stateless capitalism. What is more, the idea that there should be "more government" to fight against the excesses of capitalism verges on a theoretical power grab. What matters most is not the size of government but the nature of the normalization process.

Examining the pirate organization allows us to delve into the historically contested process of imposing norms on new, uncharted territories. The pirate organization is the missing link between the state and capital in all its forms. The pirate organization tramples on all that is lawful and legal, without in any way relinquishing the appropriation of surpluses generated by the capitalistic machine.

Chapter Four

PIRATE OR CORSAIR?

*Of course, the line that separates robbery from piracy organized by
respectable and legitimate governments has always been a very fine one.*

—Chaudhuri, *Reflections*

*The dispute about whether someone should be called a pirate or not
is really about who has the power.*

—Pérotin-Dumon, *The Pirate and the Emperor*

During the classical period, there was no linguistic distinction between pirates and looters (*corsairs*) who acted on
behalf of a town or an empire.[1] Yet, the state was already
hiring mercenaries to carry out compensatory legal sei-
zures. These types of assaults, carried out as a way to redress
past wrongs, were so common that kings and emperors
signed treaties that defined the areas in which these retali-
ations (*sulan*) were outlawed, calling these zones "asylum"
(*asulia*). It was only with the emergence of the sovereign
state and the discovery of lands outside of any preexisting
sovereignty that it made sense to use two different terms

when discussing the subject of pirates and corsairs. This linguistic nuance is not well understood or interpreted. The two pitfalls we should try to avoid are (1) lumping pirates and corsairs into the same group, or (2) contrasting them as if they were antagonistic.

A Story of Good and Evil

The corsair as the antithesis of the pirate is an oversimplification that evokes wrongly the simple separation between police and criminals. If this relationship were true, it would mean that corsairs were mandated by authorities to hunt down pirates. This is inaccurate, and it prevents us from understanding the connection between piracy and capitalistic expansion in general.

Let's take an example to illustrate our point. On June 25, 1603, Dutch Admiral Van Heemskerk seized the *Santa Catarina*, a Portuguese ship, in the Strait of Malacca. In those times, the sovereign state was growing, but nowhere in the world had it taken complete control of the ocean trade. Conflicts between European sovereigns were common, and quite often they were caused by maritime dispute. Van Heemskerk had returned a national hero after an expedition in the Arctic seas, and when he seized the *Santa Catarina*, he was working on behalf of the VOC—the East India Company for the United Provinces (now the Netherlands). The company was funded by private capital from rich Dutch merchants who also held

most of the political power within the Dutch Republic. The previous year, the United Provinces had granted the VOC an exclusive monopoly over the spice trade east of the Cape of Good Hope. The VOC was one of the first multinational companies. It was government controlled, and during its two centuries in existence, it permanently employed between ten thousand and forty thousand people. Moreover, at the beginning of the seventeenth century, the Amsterdam Stock Market was created by the rulers to facilitate the trading of securities for VOC shareholders (which, unlike today's shareholders, did not have any major decision-making power within the company). Interestingly, the first multinational company issuing tradable shares and the first stock exchange ever created came from the same roots: the sovereign state of the United Provinces.

But let's go back to what happened in the Strait of Malacca in June 1603. On behalf of the Republic of the United Provinces, Van Heemskerk attacked the *Santa Catarina*, took its cargo, and avenged his fellow countrymen who had been mistreated by the Portuguese along the spice routes. The Spanish, allies of the Portuguese, contested the legitimacy of the seizure. In their view—also shared by the church at the time—Van Heemskerk was a pirate who had pillaged a merchant ship along a route that was discovered by the Spanish, who claimed exclusive rights to the route. To the Dutch, Van Heemskerk was a valiant corsair who defended the trade interests of the republic and enforced law and order on the seas. Other nations were free

to interpret the situation in their own way. In more geopolitical terms, they could choose to become allies of Portugal or of the United Provinces.

Adopting the Flemish Perspective

In the eyes of the Spanish, all Europeans with whom they had entered into conflict between 1520 and 1650 were "pirates" in regions where the Spaniards had claimed a trade monopoly.[2] From this perspective, the English and the French who did not respect Spanish control of the route to the Americas were pirates. The issue was a legal one: on what basis can one determine whether actions are the result of piracy? At the time, international law was, at best, in an embryonic stage. It was hard for states to agree on a definition of piracy as they were still seeking recognition of their own sovereignty.[3] From the sovereign's point of view, pirates were those who did not respect the specific standards set forth by the ruler. When the Spanish and Portuguese created a trade monopoly in the West Indies, they considered any indigenous trade networks to be pirate networks. And they applied the same rationale to Europeans as well. Anyone looking to take over part of the trade market was considered a pirate.

In 1523 Captain Florin, from Normandy, captured two Spanish ships on their way back from Mexico. To the Spanish, Florin was undeniably a pirate. But to the Normans, Florin was a hero who dared to challenge Spanish supremacy,

and his exploits were worth being re-created on the stained-glass windows of the Norman church of Villequier. *Pirate*, then, is a relative term. Everyone had their pirates and at the same time could be a pirate in the eyes of others. So everyone was calling everyone a pirate. So, is the use of *pirate* and *corsair* simply a matter of perspective? That depends on what is understood by *perspective*. Let us consider the Italian perspective, à la Masaccio, the famous Florentine painter (1400–1428). Imagine you are placed before a painting, in front of the sole point where the vanishing lines meet. From the point where these lines converge, there is only one reality. You see the painting in whole. The painting offers only one interpretation according to this perspective: only one right view, other interpretations being erroneous—and any social phenomenon analyzed accordingly falls into such a Manichaeism.

If we want to increase the number of points of view, we must then turn to the Flemish perspective, à la Van Eyck (1395–1441). In one of his small paintings, titled *Saint Francis Receiving the Stigmata*, you have to stand in two different places to see Saint Francis receiving the stigmata in the foreground and then, using a magnifying glass, the view—invisible to the naked eye—of a city growing in the background.[4] With the Flemish perspective, you cannot see everything at the same time, so you must make a choice. The Flemish perspective represents a reality that superimposes landscapes at different and incompatible points of view. To see it all, to move from one layer to the next, the observer must be constantly moving.

Following this metaphor, we should not look at piracy from the Italian perspective, which would oversimplify our judgment. We should look at piracy from the Flemish perspective, which allows for different points of view and enables us to differentiate between a pirate and a corsair by running our magnifying glass over the battlefield, where multiple parties fight for territorial gain and legitimate expansion.

Letters of Marque and Reprisal and the Red Visitor

The idea that the corsair is the antithesis of the pirate is entrenched in the political history of modern European states. These states issued documents called letters of marque and reprisal, which authorized corsairs to correct past injustices by attacking the merchant ships of enemy nations. Letters of marque and reprisal were generally granted during wartimes, and they enabled corsairs to seize goods, to use force, and to take prisoners for a limited period of time. However, the near-permanent state of war in Europe made the use of these letters relatively flexible. Francis Drake, a British corsair, was far from being as quibbling as the system for letters of marque and reprisal would require it. In the 1570s, most of the raids he carried out against the Spanish were during an official period of peace. Despite formal complaints by the Spanish sovereigns, Drake's controversial actions—to say the least—did not raise any major protests in England: Drake was knighted by the queen and promoted to admiral in the Royal Navy.

At the end of the seventeenth century, the Earl of Bellomont, then colonial governor of New York, wrote the following at battle's end in a letter bound for London: "They say I have ruined the town by hindering the privateers (for so they called the pirates)."[5] Two things should surprise us in this short fragment. First, if the eradication of privateers (i.e., sea corsairs) could cause the ruin of a colonial trading post, they must have played an essential role in the economic circuit of the time. Second, it seems that the difference between pirates and corsairs was no clearer in the seventeenth century than it is today. There's no doubt that the situation was confusing for the Count of Bellomont, a wealthy man who for years had funded Captain Kidd's expeditions against French ships, before handing Kidd over to the British Crown in 1699, when Kidd was tried for piracy by a kangaroo court and hanged. Historian Violet Barbour was right to assert that "privateers were regarded as pirates, as in act they were."[6] So, the letter of marque and reprisal is, in the end, just a document produced by the state to legitimize a pirate expedition in the name of a "corsair" mandate. But this "corsairization" only has meaning from the standpoint of the sovereign who issued the letter. To other nations, these corsairs were pirates painted with a thin and contestable legal veneer.

Today, geopolitical vanishing lines converge with difficulty into a single focal point, just as they did in the past. After an American drone collided with a Chinese fighter plane over the China Sea in 2001, American computer networks were hit hard by a wave of cyberattacks. Attributed to

the Honker Union of China, a group of ten thousand cyber-pirates, the attack took aim at several hundred websites and was considered "piracy" by most Western governments.

The term *honker* (in Mandarin, *hon ke*) is derived from the words *hei ke*, the Chinese translation of the word *hacker*. *Hei ke* means "black visitor," an expression that refers explicitly to the color of the modern pirate symbol. As for the words *hon ke*, they mean "red visitor," which introduces a key nuance: the Honker Union of China is acting on behalf of the post-Communist state. From the Chinese standpoint, red visitors are not computer "pirates" but computer "corsairs." The cyberletter of marque and reprisal, reduced here to a simple semantic nuance disseminated by the Chinese government, holds no more value today in the eyes of the other nations than the letters of marque and reprisal did in Captain Kidd's time. And just like Captain Kidd, the Honker Union of China was abandoned by its former protectors: following a cyberattack against the White House's computer system, the Chinese, hemmed in by international pressure, publicly condemned the attack as an "unforgivable violation of the law." As a result of this simple statement, ten thousand "red" visitors suddenly crossed back over to the dark side, but only in a symbolic sense: the reversal of the Chinese government silenced criticism for a time, just as the public hanging of Captain Kidd did. But since 2001, the Chinese government has been suspected of orchestrating many more attacks with the help of cybercorsairs against foreign powers. For instance, the wave of attacks targeting US agencies, such as NASA, and

military contractors, such as Lockheed Martin, seems to be part of a long-term campaign that the US government has dubbed "Titan Rain."

It should come as no surprise that the US government has attempted to increase its control over cyberspace, most notably by turning cyberpirates into cybercorsairs. The InfraGard program, launched in 2001, is part of a broader initiative aimed at recruiting online corsairs to monitor the net. A recent study reported that 25 percent of cyberpirates are informants for the state. In fact, Bradley Manning, the alleged WikiLeaks source, may have been identified based on his exchanges with an undercover cybercorsair. In 2012, the press revealed that President Obama had been significantly gearing up US cyberwarfare capabilities since his election. Put simply, he assembled an army of cybercorsairs whose ultimate mission is to assert US sovereignty in cyberspace. To that end, they design cyberweapons such the Stuxnet and Flame viruses—incredibly sophisticated pieces of software that can send large plants and facilities spinning out of control, after having collected a wealth of data on enemy cyberinfrastructure.[7]

Pirate, Corsair, Pirate, Corsair, and So Forth

All corsairs are pirates, except in the eyes of the state that is sending them on a mission. As we have seen, though, the state will often abandon its corsairs if the wind turns. That being said, not all pirates are corsairs. Some pirates

form stateless hordes and attack everything in sight, with no regard for national allegiance. Between 1719 and 1722, the pirate fleet of Captain Bartholomew Roberts boarded dozens of ships on Caribbean seas, as well as along the coasts of Africa, North America, and Brazil. No historical document can prove that Roberts worked on behalf of a particular sovereign, although it was rare for a pirate to remain self-employed throughout his life.

In reality, a pirate was usually an old merchant or an old corsair or both. Francis Drake, for example, took part in many pirate expeditions before he became an English corsair. Later, he returned to the pirate life, but in 1581 he was knighted by Queen Elizabeth, which made him a corsair in the eyes of God.[8] A century later, Captain William Dampier, among many others, took a similar path, switching between the roles of corsair and pirate in the early days of a long career in which he fought in the navy against the Dutch, before retiring to a pirate community in Jamaica.[9] Biographies of cyberpirates are not much different: the red visitor was a former black visitor, who, after being abandoned by China, went back to his original color. The same was true of pirate radio DJs who were recruited by governments during both World Wars to broadcast information on their behalf.

Sometimes a pirate, sometimes a corsair. Individual roles changed. But the organizations remained the same. Individual pirates and corsairs should neither be confused nor seen as extreme opposites. But in fact, the relevant distinction should be made at the organizational level: the pirate organization differs from the corsair organization

with respect to its position vis-à-vis the sovereign state. In a constantly expanding capitalistic space, the pirate organization and the corsair organization bend sovereign norms in opposite directions, and it is important to adopt the Flemish perspective and equip ourselves with a magnifying glass to not lose track of such an essential difference.

The definition of piracy is the result of a power differential between sovereign states. As a state seeks to expand its reach, the number of individuals it considers to be pirates tends to increase. A reinforced monopoly, a more favorable trade agreement, and a more powerful navy are just some of the factors that produce pirates through exclusion, the pirate being the one living outside the boundaries defined by the sovereign. A bolder tracing of these boundaries consequently increases the intensity of the pirate threat.

Piracy is the product of geopolitics, since it appears precisely at the point where territorial space and the normative network emanating from a sovereign authority meet.

Rather than contrasting pirates and corsairs in absolute terms, we must acknowledge that the two roles are often endorsed by the same individuals at different points in time. And we should shift our attention to the much more important divide between the pirate organization and the corsair organization, which, independent of the particular individuals they employ, represent two stable patterns of social action. How positive or negative their influence is on social norms, capitalist expansion, or the development of new industries is only a matter of (Flemish) perspective.

WHAT IS THE PIRATE ORGANIZATION?

One sometimes has the impression that the flows of capital would willingly dispatch themselves to the moon if the capitalist State were not there to bring them back to earth.

—Deleuze and Guattari, *Anti-Oedipus*

Expansion is everything ... the world is nearly all parcelled out, and what there is left of it is being divided up, conquered, and colonized. To think of these stars that you see overhead at night, these vast worlds, which we can never reach. I would annex the planets if I could.

—Cecil Rhodes, founder of the chartered British South Africa Company (1889–1965), in charge of administrating Rhodesia[1]

The advances made in the sixteenth century in cartography, topography, and geodesics allowed emerging European states to mark their geographic borders and draw boundaries. This allowed states to apply norms across an entire territory. When "new" territories are explored, they are

partially uncharted. Laws are in the process of being established, and the social norms applicable to them are still in dispute. Typically, societies ask the following questions about a partially uncharted territory: Can the territory be owned? If so, by whom? By the discoverer? By the investors who funded the discovery? By the sovereign whom the discoverer is dependent upon. By those who seek to exploit the territory? Or by everyone? How can we exploit the new territory to gain legitimate profit, and how can we share it? In a nutshell, it all comes down to the creation of acceptable social norms regarding control, value creation, and value distribution.

These same questions were asked about the sea routes between the sixteenth and nineteenth centuries and about the airwaves during the twentieth century. We are asking them now in order to define the status of cyberspace and DNA, both of which are today's versions of partially uncharted territories. In the near future, we will ask the same questions regarding the status of space. Underground resources on the Moon or Mars are likely to provide enough of an incentive to trigger a discussion. Until we have come to a consensus, the new territories of capitalism will remain partially uncharted. They will stay legal, political, social, and economic gray areas where pirate organizations thrive.

From the birth of capitalism, the state has always been the most legitimate source of normalization. Penal standards, for example, define who a criminal is; fiscal standards define who a defrauder is; and business standards define

who a smuggler is. This power allowed the sovereign state to normalize and direct the flows—goods, money, soldiers, people—running through the social system. From that point on, capitalism became a matter of conquest as states sought to expand and bring new territories under their control. And with expansion came the idea of an "outside" and a "beyond," of new idealized places where new societies could be invented from scratch. This was the era of utopia, when everything was within reach, as long as you were willing to fight against the sovereignty of the state and its desires to normalize every corner of the planet.[2] The great discoveries created a rift between a territory and what lay outside it, and this rift is one of the factors that led to the emergence of the pirate organization.

Concrete Geography: Normalizing Natural Spaces

By the end of the nineteenth century, colonization brought most of the world's land mass, including the Americas and the Indies, under European control.[3] But, occasionally, organized bands would refuse to obey the sovereign. Antonio Conselheiro, a preacher, was the prototype of a renegade. At the end of the nineteenth century, he, along with his followers, rejected the rules of the Old Brazilian Republic and founded the city of Canudos in northeastern Brazil, which grew to a population of thirty thousand strong. The city took in people from all over the province of Bahia, including landless farmers, runaway slaves,

prostitutes, criminals, indigenous peoples, and Métis—the majority of which were banished from the republic. Conselheiro's band created new standards in Canudos, and the organized movement gave birth to a multitude of economic opportunities that did not come under the grip of the sovereign. A few years later, the Brazilian army attacked Canudos and massacred its people, who were in the process of becoming citizens of the Conselheiro autarkic community.

As a result of the great discoveries, states sought to normalize the new maritime routes, which opened an important chapter in the history of capitalism. During the seventeenth century, European powers issued charters to grant exclusive rights to international trade companies. These companies were created, financed, and armed by the state and were charged with organizing merchant trade from the East Indies (Southeast Asia and Oceania) and West Indies (Americas and Caribbean). In other words, these European states sought to create an economic advantage by taking control of commercial routes and normalizing them. Sovereigns used chartered companies to impose their norms upon the partially uncharted seas. Merchant organizations that refused to do business with any of these companies had to operate outside the monopolistic trade system controlled by the state. These merchants were pirates. Pursued by the navy, they set up refuge in maritime zones (Strait of Malacca, Caribbean Sea) or on land (Madagascar, Santo Domingo) abandoned by the Europeans. At this moment the first Golden Age of piracy began.

Aerial Geography: Normalizing the Analog Space

The rapid development of radio marks a similar story. Governments, especially in Great Britain, sensed that the airwaves represented a gray area that called for normalization. Shortly after the first experimental radio broadcast in 1906, states expanded their influence and imposed various levies on radio broadcasts. They granted authorization, required payments for licenses, and created rules for censorship, all of which provided the state with de facto control—economic, informational, cultural, and political—over radio. This normalization excluded many groups and individuals, and as a consequence, pirate radio was born. To escape regulations, pirate DJs would broadcast from a ship or an abandoned oil platform in international waters. This is how Radio Nordzee, a pirate radio station located on a maritime platform in the North Sea, reached the Dutch airwaves in 1963. A year later, the Dutch government claimed that the seabed below the platform was under state control, subject to its laws and regulations. A few days later, the marines and air force attacked the platform, putting an end to Radio Nordzee.

Virtual Geography: Normalizing the Digital Space

The rapid growth of the Internet is probably one of the most fascinating events in the history of capitalism. Since 1998, an American not-for-profit organization, ICANN,

has been assigning Internet domain names and regulating the network of root servers that store and distribute the information on the web. ICANN, though, has been criticized at times for its links to the US government, which are not always apparent or transparent. Every country has the right to create its own standards for regulating content on servers located on its territory. Each country can also prevent the transfer of certain content from abroad to a local terminal within its borders. China, for instance, has mastered the art of filtering digital content that is accessible from its borders. This "overcoding" of content applies to both Chinese citizens and foreign tourists. Australia was the first Western democracy to set up this type of system, which, in addition to child pornography, filters from the web thousands of pages devoted to poker, euthanasia, anorexia, Satanism, and so forth. In Denmark, a spokesperson for an intellectual property lobby recently explained how child pornography is used by states and corporations alike to achieve a much broader objective: "Child pornography is great! It is great because politicians understand child pornography. By playing that card, we can get them to act, and start blocking sites. And once they have done that, we can get them to start blocking file-sharing sites."[4] But some people reject the idea that private content should be subjected to government regulations—when public documents, such as government agency reports, are kept secret on protected servers.

Cyberpirates are organized groups that work to eliminate this marking of territory on the network by

fragmenting the segmentation established by the state. The Legions of the Underground, founded in 1994, attacked Chinese filtering systems and temporarily deactivated the function that filtered out controversial content, including Amnesty International reports on China. After a number of Western countries accused the group of cyberterrorism, they stopped their attacks on the Chinese government to avoid criminal action. More recently, pirate organizations such as Anonymous and LulzSec have begun to wage war against several government organizations and multinational corporations in the name of net neutrality.

Invisible Geography: Normalizing Infinite Spaces

The territories upon which capitalism expands do not have to be as tangible as land or the oceans. At both extremes of the visibility spectrum, the infinitely small and the infinitely large represent the future of capitalism. From genetic engineering and nanotech to space exploration, there remain several areas where the sovereign code has yet to apply. Who may modify living organisms and in the name of what? At which conditions? Who may make a profit out of it? Can organizations claim ownership of synthetic genetic sequences? Or should genetic material be considered a common good of mankind? Should all research results be made public? The question was posed recently when a modified H5N1 flu virus with high lethality for humans was engineered by a team of Dutch scientists. And, unsurprisingly, no consensual answer emerged.

The first animal—a tadpole—was cloned in 1952. At the same time, Francis Crick and James Watson uncovered the double-helical structure of the DNA molecule, thus creating the first map of a new biogenetic territory. In 1997, Dolly the sheep became the first mammal successfully cloned. As a result, scientists began to explore the possibility of cloning humans. For several years now, organizations made up of biopirates have been trying to gain a foothold in DNA research.

Although there is no serious scientific proof that a human being has ever been cloned, several well-known biopirates are working on it. DNA, in fact, is a gray area, as nearly fifty countries have yet to legislate about the cloning of humans. DNA, therefore, remains open to exploitation. Take the Clonaid project, which was launched by the Raelian sect, shortly after the birth of Dolly. For many years, Clonaid has developed a number of services related to human cloning. Due to the scientific and legal uncertainties of the project, the name of the company behind the project has been kept secret to protect its clients' anonymity. The Raelian Cloning Clinic was originally set up in the Bahamas, but due to political pressure from the French government, Clonaid moved its facility to an unspecified country in which human cloning is not explicitly outlawed. With its temporary subsidiaries in several countries, including South Korea, Israel, the United States, and Brazil, the organization is said to have many clients who are ready to pay $200,000 to clone a loved one who died too young or to clone themselves in order to achieve immortality

(metaphorically, to say the least). In late 2002, Clonaid announced the birth of the first human clone. Since then, others have made similar announcements without providing scientific proof. But isn't it only a matter of time before human cloning makes it to newspaper headlines as a fact rather than as a sci-fi cliché?

At the other end of the spectrum, the space race, started in the aftermath of the Second World War, is an ongoing normalization process. The states have yet to make stars and planets into normalized sovereign territories (in this context, planting a flag on the Moon seems trivial in retrospect). If we look at recent developments in the Brazilian, Indian, Ukrainian, Chinese, Japanese, and Korean space programs, it seems that space will be to the twenty-first century what the high seas were to the modern age.

Space, however, is not an unregulated territory. The Outer Space Treaty (1967) outlaws a sovereign state from claiming ownership over the Moon or other planets, but the treaty did not address private entities, like large companies subsidized by a state. Even so, the state does not need to "own" a territory in order to normalize it (i.e., the modern state does not "own" the airwaves). If an organization like the West India Company were landing on the Moon in a few years, we would not know what norms should govern its activities. The Outer Space Treaty sought to clarify this issue by declaring all space-related resources as the "common property of humanity." Uncertainties remain. Is it first come, first served? If so, will we live long enough to interview the first space pirates? No surprise, a handful of

privately owned companies appear to have taken a small
step forward, offering their clients the opportunity to
buy an ownership certificate for the star of their choice.
This brings to mind the golden age of conquest on the
maritime routes, except that, today, none of these private
companies control an intergalactic military fleet—and fortunately so. Still, it is only a matter of time before states and
private organizations compete for the exploitation of space
resources. In 2012, Google founder Larry Page, Microsoft's
chief software engineer Charles Simonyi, and a few other
investors announced their funding of Planetary Resources,
a space exploration start-up whose purpose is mining natural resources from asteroids. A few weeks later, SpaceX
became the first private company to send cargo into space.
For SpaceX founder Elon Musk, this is just a first step, the
ultimate objective being the settlement of human colonies
on Mars in the coming decades.

Territorial Normalization and the Pirate Organization

Every territorial expansion starts with a power struggle
between the sovereign state and its contenders. The expansion into new territories usually begins with a period of
warfare. States acquire control of a territory through the
use of their armies. European states armed their Indies
companies to normalize the oceans. The birth of cyberspace owes much to military research, which in the late

1960s financed the Arpanet project, the precursor of the Internet. The space race was fed by the Cold War, but it recently regained momentum after China made clear that manned missions to the Moon and Mars were high on its geopolitical agenda. On every territory, the state seeks to delimit, prepare the ground, draw boundaries, and define trade practices. A norm draws a line in our social space. Essentially, norms allow us to categorize behaviors into two groups: acceptable behaviors that follow the norm and unacceptable behaviors that do not. The process of normalization codes behavior based on an inclusion/exclusion. So, whenever an effort is made to normalize people's behavior, it pushes some people to the fringe. These people live within a territory, but they reject its standards. They live on the outside. They cross the line of inclusion. These renegades are "abnormal"; they are traitors in a sense, public enemies. They are confronted with a dilemma: to face stiff penalties and finally accept the norm, or to flee from the normalized territory and colonize another space with an alternative set of norms.

Conselheiro's band, the community of sailors that settled in Madagascar, Radio Nordzee, the Legions of the Underground, and the clandestine organizations working on human cloning have something of a family likeness. Working behind the scenes, these renegades run counter to the normalization process that the modern state seeks to impose every time a new territory is created. In fact, these bands share much more than a family likeness: they are all pirate organizations.

What Is the Pirate Organization?

We want to emphasize the significance of organizations in the making and workings of society, beyond the heroic and tutelary clichés about extraordinary individuals. The entrepreneur, the passionate militant, or the pirate of the Caribbean are only figures, inert masks driven by active social forces, groups, and communities. Instead of speculating about individual motives, we prefer analyzing organizational purposes, roles, actions, and outcomes. Instead of praising entrepreneurial geniuses, we prefer the concrete evaluation of networks of influence, of the organizational culture and routines, strategies, and resources—in a nutshell, the organizations that they helped create or managed.

What would Bill Gates have become without his contacts at Harvard University, his contract with IBM, and the code he adapted from Apple's early research (itself an adaptation from Xerox's research)? And would WikiLeaks really be an empty shell without Julian Assange? The organization has developed sophisticated cryptographic technologies that, combined with an impressive network of partners across the world and a deep understanding of today's digital world, have made it attractive to both whistle-blowers and media outlets. Therefore, WikiLeaks as a pirate organization and Microsoft as a doomed quasi-monopolistic corporation cannot be reduced to their individual leaders. What pushes thousands of individuals that cross the limits of normalization to form crews, fleets, communities, and societies to fight

the organized (and illegitimate in their eyes) appropriation of new spaces by territorialized states?

What is striking is the constant stubbornness to dismiss this large fringe from the social or economic reality in order to simplify and reduce the analysis sometimes on mass phenomena (globalization), sometimes on supposedly all-powerful individuals (Steve Jobs). We talk about the trends in society—the emancipation of women, urbanization, and political radicalization—but rarely about the organizations that allow these phenomena to spread into the social system. We evoke certain people as being on the forefront of social change: Johannes Gutenberg, Thomas Edison, and Coco Chanel invented book printing, the lightbulb, and haute couture, respectively. But what is really important is the implementation of specific organizations that result in the ideas of some becoming replicable and replicated social realities. Of the thousands of new ideas that emerge every day on the surface of the Earth, only a few will ever gain enough traction to become actual innovations or social facts. And eventually, those will modify the code. But their diffusion could not happen without the support of powerful organizations—whether they are for-profit corporations, nongovernmental organizations (NGOs), industry associations, government bodies, or pirate organizations. Think about this: Would we have Blu-ray without the efforts of the Blu-ray Disc Association, led by Sony, Panasonic, Samsung, Philips, and a few others? And how popular would the MP3 standard be today without Napster's pirates, who managed to attract 25

million active users to their peer-to-peer online platform between 1999 and 2001? Norms do not travel on their own.

By *organization*, we mean social groups that control resources, work toward objectives, establish transactions or links with other social entities, and develop strategies to reach these goals.[5] An organization can focus on profit and shareholders (corporation); it can be not-for-profit (association); it can be local or international (club or union), completely exclusive or inclusive (social network). Every organization has a set of inherent values that materialize in concrete forms and structures. They can be more or less in line with the state of a given society at a given time. For example, the creation of the bureaucratic organization, as defined by Max Weber, is based on skill, the depersonalization of roles, the specialization of administrative work, and the end of promotions based solely on bloodlines. The aims of an organization may benefit a small minority or a great majority. Financial, human, and technical resources can provide an organization with certain advantages, or, on the contrary, they can hinder its growth. Organizations embed themselves in society via the networks to which their members belong, which can provide them with, or deprive them of, the necessary legitimacy to carry out their actions. The principles of authority and management largely affect an organization's ability to internally set and reach its specific objectives.

The pirate organization promotes values that run counter to the norms of the state. It acts on the fringes of capitalism, in the gray areas in which norms are not fully

established and where the sovereign is unsure of actions it should encourage or discourage. The pirate organization, generally, intervenes when a sovereign first maps a territory for expansion (i.e., when the first globes were created in the sixteenth century or the human genome was mapped in the twenty-first century). The pirate organization worms its way into the sovereign state and navigates between its borders. It challenges the sovereign's control. But the pirate organization does not seek to overthrow and replace the system in place; rather, it seeks to challenge widespread norms. The pirate organization is not a revolutionary movement per se, but rather a movement that appears whenever new territories are created, and does so out of view.

The pirate organization is a social group that controls people, resources, channels of communication, and modes of transportation (for people, goods, capital, or just information). It maintains trade relations with other communities, other groups, sometimes other states, and often legitimate companies. To reach its goals, it develops new strategies that favor speed and surprise. Its goal is to adapt and improvise, to develop the appropriate means to deal with its enemy. In order to protect itself, it operates from hidden locales outside a sovereign territory. To grow, it appeals to a desire for discovery; it seeks to control parts of a territory and claims certain rights to it. To attract recruits, it plays up its outsider status, and it makes change seem possible. As long as the state strengthens its hold on norms, the pirate organization is ensured a flood of new members who feel marginalized by society.

The pirate organization proliferates in the presence of a state. This is what differentiates it from a criminal gang, which prospers when the local norms are relaxed or contain loopholes, or when the state ceases to exist in its sovereign form. What is the difference between Somali bandits who use fishing boats to attack commercial ships and their fellow countrymen who extort money from peasants? We would never think to call an extortionist a pirate—with good reason—but the members of the first group are not pirates either. Traveling in a boat does not make a pirate out of a bandit. The pirate organization, therefore, does not necessarily fit into the everyday use of the word *pirate*. Similarly, Internet users who illegally download copyrighted content are not pirates (again, this is seen from our perspective). But certainly, some of the organizations that make sure copyrighted content is freely available online would qualify as pirate organizations.

Whatever the time period, piracy exists only as such in partially uncharted territories. The pirate organization is a necessary counterpart of expanding the areas of capitalist normalization. Sometimes, the pirate organization tolerates or is even employed by the state. Sometimes it submits to state normalization in the form of a corsair arrangement. Temporary corsairization of the pirate organization precisely fills this function of partial and relative reterritorialization, enabling piratical norms to diffuse broadly within the state apparatus.

When sovereigns come to a consensus about what norms they should apply to a territory, they establish legal

boundaries, and every act of deviance from the norm is treated as criminal. Besides, an agreement across sovereign states leads to the disappearance of corsairs, or, to be more specific, it wipes out the distinction between pirates and corsairs. Clearly, pirates should not be confused with criminals, nor should corsairs, who represent their necessary counterpart within state institutions. Put differently, piracy is carried out in partially uncharted territories where the sovereign state has yet to take complete control. These territories are gray areas that do not fall under regular jurisdictions. What's more, the pirate organization often has no clearly defined nationality. If it did, it would fall under the local laws of the state, which would condemn it for trespassing, theft, or robbery. The more states refuse to grant statehood status to other political entities, the more they deprive these entities of their ability to hold territory, thus producing the gray areas that are prime for the growth of the pirate organization.

Organizations come together with an identity, a set of stated goals, and particular relationships with the normalizing state that give meaning to the development of capitalism. Understanding them avoids the simplifying image of capital as a self-devouring force without any other horizon than itself. Among the various organizational forms, one is essential for the constant evolution and recoding of capitalism. This form, perceived as irrational, abnormal, and dangerous by capitalist organizations from the legitimate milieu, appears both "necessary" and "renegade"—the pirate organization.

Chapter Six

WHERE IT ALL BEGAN:
The Pirate Organization
on the High Seas

To win new worlds,
For gold, praise and glory.

—Verse from the poet Raleigh, a hymn to maritime piracy

The pirate destroys all government and all order, by breaking
all those ties and bonds that unite people in a civil society under
any government.

—Daniel Defoe

From the viewpoint of the sovereign, piracy is used as a legal tool to ward off organized opponents. The pirate organization is the one that fights the interests of a centralized state, and the corsair does the same to that state's enemies. Yes, it is a matter of perspective, and in this respect the pirate organization is deeply embedded in the geopolitical context of any given time. Its first moments of

glory date back to the sixteenth and seventeenth centuries, when the monopolistic trade fleets of European sovereigns sailed the world's seas. Thousands of pirates thus roamed the Atlantic, the Caribbean, Africa's East Coast, the Strait of Malacca, and the Mediterranean.

The War Machine and the Pirate Organization

When a war officially ended, a corsair with letters of marque and reprisal that had expired could become a *flibustier* if he agreed to change his methods to peacefully trade legal or illegal products. *Flibustier* comes from the Dutch word *vrijbuiter*, translated literally into English as "freebooter," which means a freelance merchant. Between 1500 and 1700, thousands of flibustiers tried their luck in America. Though most flibustiers came from French ports, they were still considered to be pirates by the Spanish and Portuguese. Some of these flibustiers joined organizations such as the West India Company (WIC), which was created by the United Provinces in 1621 to run profitable expeditions to America, expeditions that increasingly resembled raiding more than trading.

Other corsairs did not want to stray from the tried-and-true methods that had made them a fortune during wartimes. Many continued to attack ships—they became pirates. They were joined by thousands of soldiers and marines who had lost their jobs after hostilities came to an end, and by sailors who did not accept their substantial

drop in pay. According to one historian's estimates, after
the signing of a peace treaty at the end of the seventeenth
century, the salaries for wartime mariners dropped by more
than 50 percent given the reduced demand for cannon
fodder.[1] Generally, in peacetime the state would renegoti-
ate with the antagonists regarding their respective exclusive trade rights. These agreements could suddenly make
the trade of certain products or navigation on certain routes
illegal, automatically extending the list of who would be
considered pirates in the future. Thus, in the years following the Peace of Utrecht in 1713, "the Spaniards repeatedly
attacked men who were cutting down trees in the bights ...
before seizing their ships, which put an end to all their
economic activities, and all sailors who were employed by
them—approximately 3,000—became pirates and overran
the seas."[2]

The Extent of the Pirate Phenomenon

We know that among the eighteenth-century pirate crews
that roamed the Caribbean, approximately 35 percent were
from England, 25 percent were from the American colonies, 20 percent were natives of the colonies, plus there
were some Dutch and French. A pirate ship had an average
crew of eighty; on the biggest ships it was not unusual for
one hundred fifty or two hundred to be on board. Compare
that with a traditional merchant ship, which carried about
twenty sailors. We know that the pirate Samuel Bellamy

took two hundred men with him, and Blackbeard took three hundred aboard *Queen Anne's Revenge*. Pirates rarely worked alone. In practice, strength in numbers gave them an advantage over better-armed adversaries. They generally organized themselves into fleets or flotillas of various sizes, but they always adapted their size and formation to the enemy. Pirates would often form squadrons of several ships. For example, Bartholomew Roberts commanded four ships that carried a total of five hundred men. The largest group recorded in the West was that of Captain Morgan, who led a fleet of more than thirty ships and two thousand men.[3]

After a successful attack, pirates would stop over in a nonhostile port. These havens of peace were scattered all over the world: Madagascar, Jamaica, Cuba, Santo Domingo, Venezuela—places where idle pirates could find cheap liquor and prostitutes, but they could also find other pirates and recruit them to replace those who died during the last battle or decided to end their career. Leaving Europe, crossing the Cape of Good Hope, reaching the Spice Islands (Moluccas) in Indonesia—in the seventeenth century, these were not easy feats. A round-trip lasted nearly two years: one exceptionally strong storm, a battle that takes a tragic turn, an unlucky encounter, an onboard epidemic, spoiled rations—any of these would have depleted a pirate crew. Often, returning to port meant a shrunken crew, several amputations, not to mention possible capture, prison, hanging without trial, or an unfortunate end in Davy Jones's locker. Here's buccaneer

Fleury describing the state of his troops during a perilous trip across the Caribbean in 1618: "In this state, it was as if our ship were abandoned ... every day we threw dead bodies off the ship, one asking for bread, another asking for water, another swearing and cursing his life ... In addition, we looked like real skeletons, or bodies that had been buried for a few days since, from the soles of the feet to the top of the head, we were covered in filth so black and persistent and sticky that we looked more like ghosts than men, which caused a stir when we arrived in the Indies ... the savages believed that we were devils."[4]

Many pirate organizations made life difficult for Her Majesty. Between 1536 and 1586, the National Archives records 361 pirate attacks, but this number accounted only for French ships operating in the Caribbean.[5] It has been estimated that in the second half of the eighteenth century, the value of goods stolen by English corsairs added up to about 10 percent of French maritime international trade.[6] Historian Marcus Rediker estimated that, between 1716 and 1726, incessant pirate attacks led to a major crisis in the British Empire and threatened the stability of international trade. In reality, the pirate organization worked on all fronts. It picked up spices in Indonesia and sold them in Cape Town or Lisbon. It took a nonnegligible percentage of the cargo of precious metal extracted from the South American mines by the Portuguese and Spanish monopolies. Moreover, the pirate organization competed with the major state-run companies by establishing parallel trade routes. For example, pirate organizations supplied the

Island of Manhattan with slaves, even though they had full knowledge of the monopolistic Royal African Company (which was founded by the Duke of York, who later gave his name to New York City).

At the time, there were approximately five thousand pirates in the Atlantic, including three thousand in the Caribbean, and a continuous presence of fifteen hundred in the Indian Ocean. In comparison, the navy had about thirteen thousand men. Depending on the year, pirates represented between 10 percent and 15 percent of the largest marine corps in the world. On land, the population of the North American colonies was approximately one hundred fifty thousand people—so the number of pirates was equivalent to 1 percent of the colonial population. At the time, some British officials feared that pirates might create their own commonwealth. Here is a quotation from a letter written by Colonel Bennet in 1718 to the Council of Trade and Plantations: "I fear that they will soon multiply for so many are willing to joyn [sic] with them when taken."[7]

Around 1800, in the China Sea, a former prostitute called Cheng I Sao worked her way up and became the head of the Confederation of the Six Flags, a pirate organization of about fifty thousand pirates. The organization's main activity was pillaging businesses controlled by the Middle Kingdom.[8] Despite the Chinese warships that were continually sent to annihilate its five hundred–ship fleet, the confederation maintained power for more than a decade. In turn, government was forced to grant a general amnesty to sea pirates in 1810.

A Real Threat: From Banditry to the Public Cause

In the classical period, bandits became pirates simply because a Barbary state on the coast of the Mediterranean did not obtain recognition from official political communities. In modern times, the states have established their borders and sovereignty, and the bandits' raids from identified neighbors become acts of war. A state cannot serve itself in its neighbor's territory with impunity for fear of creating a conflict. The law of reprisal—compensatory spoils or *sulan*—is no longer tolerated and becomes an expropriation. Pirates do not morph into corsairs as easily as before. In parallel, capitalism, through its expansion and what it includes, produces the organization of what it excludes. Integration of new territories and normalization of exchanges create the conditions for the emergence and development of a milieu favorable to capitalist exchanges. But symmetrically, it pushes to its periphery actors who organize their contestation. As a result, pirates are no longer defined by states that negate their legitimacy and denounce their actions. Instead, the pirate organization defines itself positively by differentiating its code, values, and cause from the normative will of the sovereign.

The pirate in ancient times was not recognized by anyone. He was neither the enemy of a few nor an identified common criminal. The lack of a common cause made it difficult for victims to refer to pirates or to find a reason to fight against them. International law treaties, therefore, called them enemies of everyone. However, in modern

times, pirates become organized renegades that provide a capitalist countermodel. This countermodel is both necessary and absolute in its excessiveness. Pirate organizations seek to be a radical contradiction, often too radical to succeed and convince large crowds. But occasionally, parts of their message gain acceptance and become integrated into the capitalist code. In both instances, the fate of any pirate organization is failure. Either it is wiped out by the state or it slowly dies out as its propositions are assimilated into the capitalist code (in which case it loses its raison d'être).

Extreme and necessary, the pirate organization seeks to tweak the capitalist logic that partially uncharted territories should be first monopolized, then privatized. From within the expansionist logic of capitalism, pirates stand up for a common cause they express publicly. This "public cause" feeds into the rationalization of capitalist institutions as they are renewed again and again, crisis after crisis.

In the beginning of the seventeenth century, a lively debate began about the rights and uses of new maritime territories. On the Indian Ocean, the Portuguese traded with Dutch merchants who roamed the same waters as the pirates. In his famous treatise, *Freedom of the Seas*, legal scholar Hugo Grotius wrote that waters and navigation are "free" because the sea is essentially a public good—it does not belong to anyone, and using the seas for navigation does not prevent others from doing the same. Responses came quickly from Iberic and English sovereigns, who claimed that the parts of an ocean that linked their territories together could be legally appropriated.

But it was Grotius's viewpoint that won out two centuries later. Outside of territorial waters, Grotius defended the viewpoint that no nation has the right to take possession of the open seas. Eventually, the freedom of the open seas—nowadays, more than 50 percent of all water surfaces on Earth—was achieved through a series of treaties, starting with the 1856 Declaration of Paris, which abolished privateering. The Hague Peace Conference of 1907 spelled the end of sea corsairs by forcing every sovereign to list armed vessels as military. The 1982 UN Convention on the Law of the Sea finalized the discussions by recognizing freedom of navigation on the high seas, coming around, at last, to the demands of seventeenth-century sea pirates.

Unlike the ancient version of the pirate—a simple bandit who was the enemy of the city-state—the modern pirate organization is constantly repudiated but defends a "public cause." Such a cause aims at decoding the maneuvers and norms underlying state-sponsored economic exchanges. Such decoding involves disclosing the potential inequities entailed by the sovereign code to *reveal them to the public*. WikiLeaks, in this respect, has become a master of decoding. But the public cause is also about *taking a stance in the name of the public*—a community sometimes too abstract to be able to organize and speak with one voice to the sovereign. Pirate radio became that unified voice that eventually eroded the monopoly of the BBC in the United Kingdom.

By defending a public cause, the pirate organization also publicly denounces the failings of capitalist production, and those entities that operate with the benediction

of sovereign states, such as firms and other *organizations of the milieu*—the ecological/economic environment where competition occurs according to the normalized principles of economic exchange in recognized territories. *Milieu*, in modern French, also designates the center or the middle, which contrasts with the periphery where pirates sit still before they attack. By contrast, organizations of the milieu, such as state-approved corporations operating in strategic industries (energy, defense, etc.), regulated monopolies, national technology champions, or sovereign investment funds, operate from the center of capitalism and extend the normalization promoted by states to new territories. Pirate organizations roam on the fringes of normal business; sometimes they turn coat and become corsairs, but more often than not they confront the legitimate organizations of the milieu.

The pirate organization spreads dissonant messages openly. The demands regarding the freedom of the seas, made by pirate organizations in the early seventeenth century, illustrate this idea as much as current claims for more openness on the net formulated by cyberpirates. Recognition that the high seas constitute a public good, a common heritage of mankind, represents a victory for the pirate organization—as would a similar recognition regarding cyberspace or DNA. Pirate organizations bring attention to what most people no longer see as obvious or compulsory. They put forward and defend a set of challenging values that may gather a large amount of public support. For example, the stated goal of WikiLeaks is "to make

capitalism more free and ethical." In December 2010, a poll showed that 54 percent of the French supported WikiLeaks as an organization, a level of popularity that any French politician could only dream of reaching.[9] Beyond the political content of their cause, what counts is their positioning in relation to capitalistic flows and codes. The proposals that pirate organizations make are innovative and are constantly refined in light of contemporary technologies, the net or biogenetics, airwave transmissions or space travel. What matters most is whether the public cause is accepted, and whether legitimate organizations end up endorsing it, which prompts sovereign states to grant legitimacy and legality to what was previously unthinkable.

WHY PIRACY IS NOT JUST ABOUT ECONOMICS

Everything that you are asked to do is a duty.
Everything that you refuse to do is mutiny.
—A sailor in the eighteenth-century merchant marines

The peculiar way in which pirates organize has prompted a variety of studies.[1] Historians and sociologists look into the local conditions that fostered a specific manifestation of the pirate organization. For their part, economists attempt to evaluate the costs and benefits of piracy. Their approach is limited because it is based on the idea that the pirate organization can only obey universal economic principles. If this were the case, everything would be rational among pirates, since the empire of economic reason extends over the largest kingdoms as well as the smallest duchies, over the international markets and among the highway robbers. Peter Leeson wrote a series of works that developed the rationalistic and eminently reassuring approach of pirate

organizations. Leeson sees piracy—chiefly eighteenth-century sea piracy—as an elaborate form of banditry. Here's the gist: to maintain their organization, pirates must set up mechanisms to control the crew by preventing theft and conflicts. These mechanisms must also maximize profits. The pirate organization operates on the fringes of the legalized and state-controlled world. Therefore, it must establish tenable principles of behavior, internally, since it cannot appeal to the state and its courts in the event of a conflict.

Economics Alone at the Helm?

Most sea pirates came from the hierarchically structured merchant marine. At the top was the captain of the ship, who controlled all aspects of the crew's lives, including food distribution, chores, salaries, and discipline. Therefore, for the legal transport of goods, ship owners selected the best merchant marine captains who believed in doing their jobs by any means necessary, especially when investors were involved. These backers gave the captain absolute power to get rid of crew members who showed the slightest hint or intention of theft or laziness. The captain imposed order. He was protected by laws that authorized leg irons and corporal punishment. To keep the captain's power in check and to ensure a safe expedition, investors made the captain a minority shareholder. The captain received a share of the profits along with his fixed salary as a sailor. To ensure social control and profit, investors would often

choose captains who were close contacts or whom they had a direct family tie with. If the captain did not arrive safely in port, he would lose his initial investment, the return on his investment, and the respect from his family and peers.

It was not rare for captains to abuse their authority for their own benefit. In fact, when sailors were mistreated by dishonest captains, they would often leave for other jobs. As the quotation in the epigraph of this chapter says, a basic sailor must obey—if not, he is seen as a mutineer. The threat of hardship and poor treatment was constant. The captain was all the more likely to use violence and intimidation if he had not been able to choose his own crew, and vice versa. Loyalty and trust therefore were the exceptions to the rule. Piracy was then an attractive option for mistreated sailors.

For its part, the pirate organization responded differently to economic requirements. First, given that the cost of acquiring or investing in the pirate ship was close to zero (i.e., it was stolen), the pirate organization did not adhere to the separation of economic tasks as the merchant marines did. So, any decisions about food, chores, salaries, and rewards, as well as attack strategies and escape plans, required a different chain of command. The most adopted system involved two levels of control. First, all members of the organization elected the captain, democratically. The same process was used to remove and replace captains. Second, power and authority could be spread among the crew.

Whereas in the merchant marine there were two co-existing populations (officers and sailors) held together by

authority, on board a pirate ship, the community was one and united. However, to guarantee everyone's rights and to maintain the cohesion of the crew, the ship's command was shared by two complementary positions: the captain and the quartermaster. The captain was essentially in charge of major maritime operations. But in the event of an attack or a joint mission with other allied vessels, the distribution of rations and booty and the management of internal conflicts were the responsibility of the quartermaster. For many, the eighteenth-century sea pirate organization adhered to the democratic separation of powers, long before states did. When a captain was deposed after a majority vote due to, say, a lack of courage, a bad decision, or any other shortcoming, the quartermaster was often elected as the captain's replacement. This would often give rise to competition between crew members vying for the quartermaster position. Unlike the authoritative merchant marine captain, whose privileges included getting the best cabin and the best food, the pirate ship captain did not receive any preferential treatment. His cabin (if he had one) was not private, and he ate the same food as his comrades. This equality also applied to the quartermaster. In fact, it was stipulated in the charters or articles that set out the rules of living and sharing within most pirate organizations. This type of agreement was called the *custom of the coast* and was based on the practices of the pirates of the Caribbean. The different codes of conduct adopted and amended by pirate communities are very similar. As the code used by Captain Roberts and his crew shows, harmful activities that could

potentially lead to conflicts or that could negatively affect the expedition were not tolerated. In particular, alcohol, gambling, and sex were prohibited.[2]

EXCERPTS FROM CAPTAIN ROBERTS'S CODE

Every man has a vote in the affairs of moment, and equal title to fresh provisions or strong liquors, at any time seized, and may use them at pleasure, unless a scarcity makes it necessary, for the good of all, to vote a retrenchment.

Every man to be called fairly in turn, by list, on board of prizes … but if they defrauded the company to the value of a dollar in plate, jewels, or money, marooning was their punishment.

No person to game at cards or dice for money.

The lights and candles to be put out at eight o'clock at night: if any of the crew, after that hour still remained inclined for drinking, they were to do it on the open deck.

To keep their piece, pistols, and cutlass clean and fit for service.

No boy or woman to be allowed amongst them. If any man were to be found seducing any of the latter sex, and carried her to sea, disguised, he was to suffer death.

To desert the ship or their quarters in battle was punished with death or marooning.

No striking one another on board, but every man's quarrels to be ended on shore, at sword and pistol.[3]

Following a take, the quartermaster had to respect the accounting principles accepted by the entire crew before

setting sail. For example, the carpenter and surgeon were paid first because of the indispensable service they provided. Next, the wounded, due to the hardships they suffered, were paid according to a precise code. They received a larger share than their crewmates, thus instituting one of the first forms of social insurance. For example, if a crew member lost his right arm, he received three times the pay of the surgeon, but if he lost an eye, he received half. From what remained of the take, the captain received a double share, each crew member received an equal share, and young boys received half. If a ship was taken, each crew member had to swear—often on the Bible, but also on other texts—that he had not taken anything so that each could then receive an equal portion of the booty. In addition to the equal profit sharing, a bonus system was often used for the bravest pirates in order to reward individual initiative. All in all, the discipline that pirates voted on and imposed on themselves was stricter and more stringent than the rules they imposed on their prisoners.

Pirates' Norms Travel Fast

Advances that took modern governments several centuries to institutionalize were established by the pirates of the Caribbean and Madagascar: democratic elections of leaders, separation of powers, equality between members, and an early form of social insurance. Leeson and others see these institutions as an economic necessity. They

were developed on the need for internal coherence. For the pirate organization that faced a lot of uncertainty and could not resort to legal justice, these advances were essential. As Leeson says, "No outside authority centrally designed, directed, or imposed democracy on pirate society. Pirates' criminal interest led them to adopt this system without external prodding."[4] The economic handling of the pirate organization and its cruel reality—the violence inflicted on those who did not respect the rules—intensify its abnormal, monstrous, and criminal side.

There is always an economic explanation for everything in the pirate legend. Some economists have used signaling theory to dissect the Jolly Roger, the black pirate flag with the white skull and crossbones. It would seem that the acceptance of emancipated slaves, who were treated as equals, is based on a simple cost-benefit calculation. Looking back, Leeson ascribes purely economic motivations to all pirates' decisions. His economic approach sees these things as logical consequences that resulted from the costs associated with the running of the organization: its banishing, its capital structure, its riskiness, and so forth.

We are tempted to reverse this logic and see the pirate organization as the consequence of the wide-reaching presence of more democratic, more modern, and more egalitarian principles in society. In a way, the banishment of the pirate organization is not the reason why it establishes different principles for living and distribution. Rather, the reverse is true. The pirate organization is pushed to the fringes because it creates dissonant rules for living and

alternative theories of ownership in the gray areas that
have yet to be normalized. The poor treatment of merchant
marine sailors, the slave trade, inequality in growing rev-
enues, undue appropriation of profits by military force, the
weakening of monarchic authority, and the dissemination
of Enlightenment ideas—all these could just as easily be
the reasons behind the exodus of a band of sailors and the
rise of liberalist ideas about property and trade that were
held by doctors and captains.

Furthermore, if universal economic principles were dic-
tating how pirates organize themselves and act, we should
observe quite a homogeneous pirate organization across
the globe. However, although the pirate organization publicly contests everywhere the appropriation of gray areas,
it takes on different forms in different parts of the world.
For instance, a pirate fleet could range from a dozen ships
in the Caribbean islands to hundreds of ships in Asia. Also,
codes differ from one region to another. Hence, absent
some other political and institutional motivations, it is hard
to understand why the same universal economic rationality
would yield different outcomes in different seas.

Despite its flaws, an economic analysis can help to
explain the existence and operations of the pirate organization. Analyzing the relations between means, chain of
command, and rules for distributing booty is indispensable
and very instructive. The pirate organization needs ships
to sail along the gray areas of an expanding world. It needs
men and resources to continue its activities. It has to broadcast the public cause it defends, which is that of a legitimate

expropriation of the sovereign and its allied corporations, rendered necessary, according to pirates, when the latter ignore the broader interests of the community.

In spite of it all, we think that a complete analysis of the pirate organization needs to go beyond a purely economic perspective because it is economic logic that the pirate organization fights against. We need other explanations. Because the pirate organization thrives on the fringes of partially uncharted territories, it participates in their normalization, albeit indirectly. The pirate organization does not hide within the interworking of the system. It stands on the surface, flies a recognizable flag, catches people's attention, and arouses the fury of sovereign-protected owners. It meddles in the gray areas and keeps on countering organizations of the milieu at every turn. The pirate organization is truly a force that acts out against capitalistic overcoding. It tries to clear the paths of incessantly repeated normalization but keeps advocating publicly for changes in perspective.

Chapter Eight

THE PIRATE ORGANIZATION
ON THE AIRWAVES

Piracy on the airwaves is a form of anarchy.

—Hugh Jenkins, president of the Labour Communications
Committee (UK), 1966

The BBC: now enjoying an international reputation, the British Broadcasting Corporation has long been the sworn enemy of a series of illegal companies previously known as "pirate radio stations."[1] The first radio broadcasts created a new, uncharted territory for capitalism to expand into. While in the aftermath of World War I, "the media experienced immense popularity, ... most of its basic principles— its technical characteristics, its daily use, its standards, its regulations and perhaps, above all, its entire economy— remained to be determined."[2]

The Fight Against Pirate Radio

The BBC was founded in 1922 as a government monopoly. But Britain's grip on this partially uncharted territory did not please everyone. Starting in 1928, pirate radio stations transmitted radio broadcasts from makeshift ships. They made sure to moor their ships far enough from the British coast to elude legal prosecution. Most pirate radio stations believed that radio broadcasting as imposed by the monopolistic BBC was unacceptable. Why not allow several stations to broadcast on different wavelengths so that people could choose their own program? Why impose an educational goal when radio could be highly entertaining, make people think, allow listeners to express themselves, to dance with friends in the middle of the living room? Why only broadcast classical music when you could also offer bebop, swing, and later rock and roll? The BBC would come up against hordes of pirate radio stations, which continued to push the limits of radio broadcasting for another forty years.

In 1930, pirates created the International Broadcasting Corporation (IBC) to contest the BBC's model. The IBC forged partnerships with many pirate radio stations throughout Europe in order to propose alternative programming rights under the noses of BBC representatives. The IBC proposed a radically different model that favored varied programming and contemporary music. In this model, the best programs on sister pirate radio stations were compiled and rebroadcast. They were tailored to a

specific audience using relay antennas. The programs were picked based on location and adapted to the sociological traits of each city and suburb. In contrast with the BBC, which was always live, the IBC prerecorded parts of programs, which were combined and rebroadcast in a number of geographic markets. The IBC was funded by advertising, and it enabled its founder, Leonard Plugge, to get rich quick given the success of its programs.

Pirate radio stations that popped up after World War II fine-tuned their methods for evading standards and regulations. For example, Radio Mercur, founded in the 1950s, broadcast from a ship located in international waters, but the ship itself was registered in Panama, was funded with Swiss money, and was rented to a company established in Liechtenstein. It was almost impossible for authorities to take legal action against radio pirates of this type.

The BBC and its defenders were adamant in their belief that broadcasting beyond the borders of the sovereign state should be banned. Such a ban eliminated any possibility of broadcasting a program outside the country in which it was produced. Obviously, this prohibition made no sense, since radio waves, by their very nature, cross the physical boundaries of countries and technically cannot be stopped by force. Moreover, the British Crown, famously, bent its own rule when it ordered pirate stations to broadcast anti-Nazi propaganda outside the United Kingdom at the outset of World War II. This is how the IBC was recruited by the BBC in the 1940s, when British secret services were discretely buying up airtime on Radio Luxembourg, the

main pirate radio station in the mid-twentieth century to broadcast Chamberlain's speech on the German airwaves. This kind of practice did not occur only during wartime: in 1962, Radio Mercur was dissolved by the Danish government, which at the same time had recruited a large number of its speakers to host programs within the national broadcasting association. Therefore, radio also had its corsairs.

In addition to the protection of the sovereignty of the national territory, the BBC used another argument to justify its fight against pirate radio: the defense of intellectual property. It's true that pirate radio stations broadcast music without paying all record company royalties. But for most innovative record companies that invested in rock and roll, pirate radio was the only means to reach a larger audience, since the BBC categorically refused to broadcast what it considered to be anarchistic music. Even as they complained about not receiving royalties, record companies still managed to send out previews of their new records so that listeners could get to know them. These companies were the unofficial instigators of a vast pirate enterprise that boosted both their reputation and sales, even as they fought alongside the government and the BBC. The BBC also found itself caught in the web of its own antipirate talk: in order to protect their sales, the record companies authorized the BBC to broadcast only twenty-two hours of musical programming per week, while the majority of pirate stations were playing upwards of ten hours of rock and roll each day.

Successive waves of capitalist expansion into new territories create a series of gray areas from where pirate organizations can diffuse and defend their public cause. In their
own quest for political or economic advantage, organizations of the milieu sometimes compromise by adopting the
pirate way behind the scenes while publicly opposing it
(e.g., think of record labels siding with the BBC regarding
copyright issues while making sure that their latest releases
are broadcast on pirate radio stations). Record labels put the
BBC in a corner and participated in its commoditization,
ending its monopoly and the direct control of the sovereign
over its programs. Absent pirate radio, the entertainment
and media industries could have taken a very different
path, which ironically could have prevented them from
dominating the sphere of cultural production throughout
the twentieth century—at least until the rise of cyberspace
in the late 1990s.

Chapter Nine

THE PIRATE ORGANIZATION
AND THE MONOPOLIST

*Traditionally, the granting of a trade monopoly ... is a power that
the sovereign exercises over his territory, its citizens, a power that
is then extended to the territory and the colonized people. The very
concept of law is closely linked to that of territoriality.*

—Soderberg, *Hacking Capitalism*

*To eliminate piracy on a larger scale, however, trade monopoly
had to be given up altogether.*

—Pérotin-Dumon, *The Pirate and the Emperor*

To exploit the resources of a new territory, states define
which organizations can operate, embody, and convey the
norms of exchange as well as determine property rights, the
nature of risks, and the sharing of returns on investment.
Historically, monopolies bring together capitalist territori-
alization with the normalization of trade. Often, monopolistic organizations are granted sovereign charters by the
state in order to make normalization possible. The East
India Companies, for example, were chartered companies,

and so was the BBC. Both helped sovereigns to normalize partially uncharted territories.

On the other hand, the pirate organization champions a public cause in opposition to the sovereign's norms. It is a renegade form of economic action from within the limits of capitalism itself. It disputes the basic assumptions of capitalism—levying of tax and capturing of profits—the tenets that characterize the monopoly state and its offshoot, the oligopoly state. The pirate organization claims other rights for economic exploitation, without "legally" defining a territory or establishing property rights.

Route to the Indies, Commercial Monopoly, and the Birth of Capitalism

In 1498, Vasco da Gama sailed from Portugal around the Cape of Good Hope and opened the route to the East Indies. Over the next fifteen years, the Portuguese court sent a series of armed armadas to the Indies in order to eliminate Muslim trade throughout the area and prepare the ground for the Portuguese arrival. This period marked the beginning of the reign of a new form of economic organization: between the sixteenth and eighteenth centuries, the modern European state established the trade monopoly as a fulcrum for capitalistic expansion. In particular, the Portuguese Crown wanted to capitalize on new trade opportunities that were opened up to the east by Vasco da Gama. To do this, the Portuguese Crown granted a royal

charter to Carreira da India, a trade organization, giving it the exclusive right to import spices into Europe.[1]

It was only at the beginning of the seventeenth century that other European powers entered into the race to set up a monopoly with the support of the Indies companies. This is how, in 1602, the United Provinces granted the VOC a twenty-one-year monopoly on trade with the regions lying east of the Cape of Good Hope. For many historians, the VOC remains the archetype for the "merging of sovereignty and trade monopoly—that is to say the strict integration of the political, military and market sectors."[2] Monopolies are a very powerful force of normalization in the modern age. These large corporations employ tens of thousands of employees whose mission is to conquer new territories. Historically, the flow of people—soldiers and merchants—who came out of this new form of organization were controlled through a series of norms of unprecedented complexity: international laws for managing trade conflicts, fiscal treatises for charging a surplus, administrative norms for company governance, accounting standards for circulating assets, rules for training troops and guidelines for combat, rules of behavior for encounters with aboriginal populations, stock market directives for financing the development of large corporations, and even rules for recruiting sailors.

Most of the norms governing monopolistic trade were a novelty at the time, as were most of the institutions that facilitated their use. The opening of the Amsterdam Stock Market in 1611, the founding of the Siegen military academy in 1616, and the use of risk calculations by insurance companies

are just a few obvious examples. For almost two hundred years, large European monopolies would continue to dominate international trade by following these same principles.

The common view of capitalism now is that it is essentially based on free competition. But is it? From the seventeenth century on, monopolies have been the rule, and free trade has usually been the exception. When historians analyze the modern era in comparison with other eras, they conclude that the (relative) freedom of trade has had a long history, and that trade regulations established by the modern state were the true innovation.[3] In any event, at the beginning of the capitalist era, monopolies and other sovereign privileges spearheaded the globalization of flows. They constitute the terrain from which capitalism evolves.

Christopher Hill rightly observes that "pirates exterminate those who bought privileges from a State."[4] In fact, pirates seem to defend the right to venture off on their own, to follow their own standards, and to benefit from the profits. In the modern age, the monopoly was a privilege that excluded private initiatives. This led to the quick ruin of well-established merchants and consequently gave rise to two phenomena: some companies stood up against monopolies by establishing a parallel and illicit trade route, and some tried to violently take over part of the flows from a monopoly. From the perspective of the sovereign state, both types of response were considered piracy. The growth of the pirate organization in the seventeenth century therefore cannot be separated from the normalization process of world trade carried out by the sovereign states.

Analog Revolution, Pirate Radio Stations, and the Monopoly of the BBC

Between the early 1920s and the late 1960s, the BBC defended its monopoly, claiming that other stations created interference on BBC airwaves. By claiming interference, the BBC also rationalized prohibiting foreign stations from broadcasting into British territory. AT&T made similar arguments in the United States when it claimed a commercial monopoly over transmissions received using AT&T-built equipment. In 1924, AT&T sued the New York–based pirate station WHN. AT&T won the case, but in the eyes of many the decision was not completely legitimate, so the court ruling was only partially applied. As many technical studies done at the time showed (in particular those of Ronald Coase), the interference argument proved to be completely false and was used only to protect monopolies that were increasingly difficult to defend. In the case of the BBC, this monopoly was upheld for another ten years via a royal charter granted in 1927, much like the one used three centuries earlier that upheld the East India Company's monopoly. The BBC charter expired in 1967.

The British government created the BBC monopoly as a way to shape the emerging industries that would soon rely on the airwaves as a communication channel, which the authorities likened to "ether." The BBC served as a vehicle to diffuse norms and standards that would shape the political, sociological, economic, and cultural dimensions of radio broadcasting for the decades to come. The

first standard: the BBC is the central authority that broadcasts sovereign-endorsed programs throughout the British Commonwealth. Second standard: the objective is to educate the public. Third standard: only receivers certified by the postal service can receive BBC programs, and listeners must pay an annual fee to renew the license, which authorizes them to listen to the programs. The money collected was used to fund the programs, which, at the time, were free of advertising. If necessary, postal inspectors had the right to enter households, without warning, to check that listeners were following the rules. Fourth standard: the programs must inform people about a certain "noble" culture, especially through religious and classical music programming. The BBC recommended listening to entire programs in silence and in a seated position, with the main focus on the radio—in no way should household chores interfere with your listening while the BBC was teaching you. On Sundays, the BBC would cease broadcasting most of the day to encourage listeners to go to church.

After forty years of fierce fighting against pirate radio, the BBC's monopoly finally came to an end in 1967. As a result, the BBC adopted some of the norms proposed by the pirates. After pirate radio stations poached most of its radio hosts, the BBC created Radio One, a station that offered a wider variety of programming, more current music, and a more liberal tone. As Adrian Johns explained, "as of 1967, the BBC became one among many ... The irony is that it then found the critical and skeptical voice it had been missing ... the virtues of the BBC only came to light at the end

of its monopoly."[5] Surprisingly, the renewed radio broadcasting industry, as it has existed since 1967 and as most of
us know, falls within the model proposed by the pirates
in the first half of the twentieth century—a model against
which major monopolies fought aggressively at the time.

Digital Economy, Cyberhackers, and Capitalism in the Third Millennium

Today, cyberpirates are opposing the normalization of
data sharing and the monopolistic control of digital space.
Many companies, especially from the music or film industries, defend their territory and therefore the exploitation
of their property rights. In mid-January 2012, two important events marked the opposition between the two con-
ceptions of information exchange on markets. The US
Congress postponed the vote on the Stop Online Piracy Act
(SOPA), promoted by many firms, whereas other organizations were demonstrating against this act. As the bill proposed to shut down sites within and outside US territory
that contain any content protected by American intellectual property rights, opponents saw it as a prohibition to
exchange cultural content freely on domains that belong
to mankind in general and not to any particular territorial
state. Wikipedia, which embodies this idea of digital common good, displayed a black home page and blocked access
to its content for twenty-four hours in a move to protest
against the act. About 160 million people worldwide saw

the site's banner that day. Google reported to have received 7 million signatures for a petition opposing the law.

The second event is the spectacular arrest of Kim Dotcom and the turning off of his company Megaupload. After Napster made peer-to-peer exchanges possible for music, Megaupload stirred things up with the diffusion of TV programs and films, centralizing content with and without legal protections and enabling streaming, questioning laws regarding intellectual property and the exchange of cultural content. Just as in the regular TV crime shows Megaupload stored in its servers, in the end the FBI stepped in to forcibly catch Kim Dotcom on the New Zealand island where he had found refuge. The FBI also seized the vessels of his computer-geek fleet. The Megaupload affair was seen by many as an act of compensation from the state toward the unsatisfied proponents of the SOPA, an indication that the sovereign state is firmly resolute in its intention to crack down on the organizations that unduly benefit from rights they do not own. Both events highlight the importance of continuously recoding the laws that govern intellectual property and the creation and distribution of cultural goods.

The actions of the pirate organization on the net take many forms. Pirates both create and distribute free software and content. They change the net in general. For example, a hacker was behind the invention of e-mail as a means to connect users of terminals in various locations. A researcher working on the Arpanet military communications project—the predecessor of the Internet—once discretely modified the source code of several software

applications developed by the military research agency in 1971 in order to send the first e-mail remotely using the @ symbol "mainly because it seemed like an elegant idea."[6] The dream of an open digital world almost became a reality in the 1970s after a court ruled that AT&T (again!) was in violation of antitrust laws, which prohibited the company from selling UNIX software (the company agreed to terms but eventually started selling it again in 1982). UNIX is an operating system that enables software and hardware to run together on a computer. The free distribution of UNIX in the 1970s enabled users to easily modify the source code to meet their needs. These changes significantly improved upon the original version produced by AT&T, which nevertheless attempted to enforce its patent for UNIX starting in 1982 in order to collect royalties and prevent future modifications without compensating the thousands of developers who voluntarily developed the program. In response to AT&T's uncompromising attitude, the hacker movement organized itself and took on quite a different dimension. Nothing has really changed. Pirates are still fighting to revive the slightly "crazy" idea of an open and free digital territory that would not fall under the complete control of governments and monopolies.

Once again, the alliance between a sovereign state and monopolistic organizations nurtures a milieu that delineates the norms applicable to a partially uncharted territory. And once again, this situation gives rise to organized piracy by excluding groups of people and pushing them to the fringes. These pirate organizations stand up against

the state and its accompanying legitimate corporations. We may even wonder whether AT&T, Microsoft, and Google are to American sovereignty what the VOC was to the sovereignty of the United Provinces—that is, instruments of normalized capitalist deterritorialization disguised as corporations. In early 2010, a member of Hillary Clinton's staff, following an attack by Chinese cybercorsairs against Google, told the press that the American Department of State "is not the armed hand of Google for foreign policy." The simple fact that it appeared necessary to release this statement speaks volumes about the internal dynamics of capitalist expansion, as it is perceived by the upper echelons of the state. Months later, it would be revealed that Google had been working hand in hand with the highly secretive National Security Agency (NSA) to investigate the origins of this attack, which had but minor consequences. And in 2012, a court ruled that Google did not have to disclose the exact nature of its relationship with the NSA.[7] Any resemblance with the VOC's state-supported conquest of the high seas in the seventeenth century would be, of course, purely coincidental.

The Inner Tension Between Capitalism and Liberalism

Sea pirates fighting for the end of the East India Company's monopoly? Pirate radio struggling against the BBC's monopoly? Early cyberpirate communities targeting the

monopolies of AT&T and Microsoft? For those who think that capitalism and liberalism go hand in hand, this must come as a shock: capitalism does not exactly expand into new territories using the invisible hand of free market economics, but rather the very visible hand of state monopolies.

In this respect, the list of corporations recently targeted by Anonymous, the pirate organization supportive of Julian Assange's WikiLeaks, is puzzling. Visa and MasterCard? A combined 95 percent market share worldwide. Monsanto? A 95 percent market share of genetically modified soybeans in the United States. In a 2010 interview in *Forbes*, a journalist asked Assange whether he would call himself a free market proponent. Assange's answer was crystal clear: "Absolutely. I have mixed attitudes towards capitalism, but I love markets. Having lived and worked in many countries, I can see the tremendous vibrancy in, say, the Malaysian telecom sector compared to the U.S. sector ... In Malaysia, you have a broad spectrum of players, and you can see the benefits for all as a result."[8]

Do capitalism and monopolies work badly together? Well, that depends. What is competitive today may become monopolistic tomorrow, and vice versa. One of the essential reasons capitalism spread in the modern era using monopolies is because they represented the best organizational arrangement to accelerate the circulation of flows through the action of a sovereign state. The apparently ironclad relationship that currently exists between capitalism and free trade is in reality an unsound opinion that is based on historical shortsightedness. Free trade is not a

necessary cog in the capitalist machine. During the first two centuries of capitalism, monopolistic trade organized under the aegis of the sovereign state is what enabled deterritorialization of flows to increase and intensify. Interestingly, many industries that are core to our society grew out of monopolistic regimes.

Another prominent monopoly in the seventeenth century was the one granted to the Stationers' Company through the 1662 Licensing Act, which is the ancestor of the 1709 Statute of Anne, also known as the first copyright act in history designed by a monopolistic coalition of publishers. The Licensing Act was a law passed by the British sovereign in order to control book circulation and contain harmful pamphleteering. Copyright law then emerged out of a monopolistic framework that was aimed at nothing more than censorship, as envisioned by Queen Mary I in 1557, when she first devised an arrangement "where the London guild would get a complete monopoly on all printing in England, in exchange for her censors determining what was fit to print beforehand."[9] Fortunately, the subsequent Statute of Anne reversed some of the most antisocial provisions of the Stationers' Company charter by putting an end to the perpetual character of copyright protection, thereby curbing the privileges of the monopoly. By specifying an expiration date for intellectual property protection, the 1709 charter partly displaced the problem and postponed the conflict between the sovereign and the pirates. Now that innovation circulates so much more rapidly, many

think the state should reconsider—that is, shorten—the duration of intellectual property protection.[10]

Capitalism and free trade are not intrinsically linked. In fact, free trade represents only one method of capitalism. Clearly, this conclusion has tremendous implications for current political discussions about the future of capitalism—but also about the future of anticapitalism as debated heatedly among antiglobalization movements.

THE PIRATE ORGANIZATION
IN CYBERSPACE

Governments of the Industrial World, you weary giants of flesh and steel, I come from Cyberspace, the new home of Mind. On behalf of the future, I ask you of the past to leave us alone. You are not welcome among us. You have no sovereignty where we gather.

—John Perry Barlow, "A Declaration of the Independence of Cyberspace," 1996

Our age is the age of cyberspace. It, too, has a regulator. This regulator, too, threatens liberty. But so obsessed are we with the idea that liberty means "freedom from government" that we don't even see the regulation in this new space. We therefore don't see the threat to liberty that this regulation presents.

—Lawrence Lessig, "Code Is Law," 2000

The struggles between states and pirate organizations in the digital territory are complex, but the questions that arise from this new struggle are reminiscent of the Golden Ages of sea piracy and pirate radio: if the net is a territory, what should its boundaries be? How should they be

defined and by whom? Who should control cyberspace and the information circulating therein? How should we share the legitimate profits derived from deterritorialized capital, which accumulates on the net mainly in the form of software, information databases, and viral celebrity? For software companies, the exploitation of their property rights under the form of licenses to users fuels their continuous investments into upgraded versions of their products. Pirate organizations contest the public benefit of such proprietary systems; for them software should be free to use, as it is akin to a language that belongs to humanity.

Software as Enclosure and the Freeware Ideal

Software has wormed its way into our lives. It determines, plans, and controls the behavior of computers, cars, and electronic devices of all kinds. Software organizes and controls our movements on roads and railways and in the air, the production and broadcasting of music via digital channels, the presentation of information using office suite software, the way in which plates are dried in a dishwasher, and automatic buy-and-sell market transactions. Software is a summary of replicable procedures within a coherent set of contexts in which specific tasks are to be performed. Software lets us carry out complex operations that do not specifically require human intervention. Software encloses code—a collection of instructions written in computer language. Different paths of code can be used to achieve the same outcome, just as

different sentences can render the same meaning. However, once one of the many alternative coding schemes has been set in proprietary software, its content cannot be changed anymore and its use becomes confining.

Although most software is "customizable," preprogrammed software is the standard, as it allows us to accomplish tasks as quickly as possible. For an entire community of individuals, proprietary software is a closed system that limits free expression. Think about the way in which a software application like PowerPoint has radically changed the running of organizations over the past twenty-five years. Many employees spend the bulk of their workdays writing, rereading, correcting, and editing PowerPoint presentations. They wind up thinking in terms of lists, bullet points, and subpoints: each idea is broken down into two or three chunks of information backed up by a recent example, a comical image, or a joke, while the presenter goes to great pains to ensure that the audience does not suffer "death by PowerPoint."

Many groups of computer specialists have come together to form cyberpirate organizations. Their public cause is twofold: to denounce the reductionist and expressionless aspect of software; and to decode the highly profitable economic model of software producers by proposing free and accessible alternatives that can be enhanced by the community. Interestingly, Richard Stallman, the leader of the Free Software Foundation, explained once that exclusive property (most notably that related to software) "made pirates out of what would be merely good, helpful neighbors."[1]

The Birth of the Cyberpirate Organization

In the 1970s, the first organizations of computer activists, such as the Homebrew Computer Club, did not involve "pirates," so to speak; rather, these organizations were made up of computer buffs who were looking to improve existing equipment—they were "hackers." There are important differences between cyberpirates and hackers. While cyberpirates aim to establish alternative norms in a digital territory, hackers merely tweak a technology's purpose or function (typically, a bored hacker could try to build a satellite receiver out of a broken microwave oven).[2] Unlike pirates, hackers do not attempt to formulate political, economic, or legal demands—they just want to have fun, enhance their technical skills, and gain peer recognition. Besides, hackers are interested in particular markets rather than territories, each of which can host multiple markets. For instance, cyberspace hosts markets for virtually any type of product, ranging from cookbooks to technical devices for lawnmowers or electric shavers. Often, the hacker is specialized in a particular type of device, such as satellite receivers. A pirate, on the other hand, seeks to modify the norms of cyberspace. Put simply, hackers tinker with technologies, while pirates influence the norms embedded in territories.

A recent study by Jarkko Moilanen showed that 90 percent of hackers have membership in a single "hackerspace," providing evidence that hacking is an activity focused on specific products.[3] Hacker Mitch Altman, for instance, has devoted the last decade of his life to the refinement of a one-button

universal remote control used for turning off any television. The same study also demonstrated that hackers' primary interest is in building new objects, typically by changing the functions of preexisting products. Roughly speaking, pirates could thus be seen as higher-order hackers. It is important to note, however, that many early cyberpirates started their career as hackers in the 1970s and that the careers of pirates begin in hacker communities.

Hackers in the 1970s were interested mainly in hardware, a term that refers to all hard components of a computer terminal (processor, motherboard, etc.). After the first computers were networked, the upheavals in the computer industry brought hope. Also, the most utopian dreamers among these pioneers were already picturing themselves in a world where information would become freely available to all, where everyone could communicate with everyone else, and where the computer would offer everyone the possibility of creative expression independent of the traditional capitalistic norms, large corporations, or the state. This dream would become true thanks to the proliferation of personal computers, facilitated by the discoveries of the Homebrew Computer Club, some members of which later became the first cyberpirates. Among the early members of the club was Steve Jobs, the former CEO of Apple, who for a long time flew the pirate flag out in front of the company's head office. In 1976, the club received a document accusing the members of illegally using the BASIC program—that is, using the software without authorization from its creator and without paying royalties. The author

of this letter was Bill Gates, a savvy geek who was willing
to push his peers to the fringes of a new territory.

The Dilemma of Digital Sovereignty

Opening proprietary software is not the only objective of
cyberpirates. The creation of cyberspace prompted pirate
organizations to fight against a new form of sovereign
normalization. In the 1980s, network connections were
the privilege of universities, government agencies, and
pirate organizations that were thriving while fighting with
the state. In 1988, *Phrack*, a widely distributed magazine
among hackers that specialized in underground comput-
ing, published a list of pirate organizations found in the
digital territory. The publication counted 131 in the United
States. Some organizations had only a handful of members; others, dozens of apprentice pirates who, a decade
later, would train a large part of the pirate contingent on
how to operate on a large scale on the democratized net
that had become available to the masses. The name of
these organizations already brought to mind an aggressive
stand toward the state and monopolistic companies in the
telecommunications sector (e.g., Apple Mafia, Bell Shock
Force, IBM Syndicate, NASA Elite, Phortune 500, OSS,
The Administration, Anarchy Inc.). It goes without say-
ing that the development of these organizations, in number
and in size, was gaining ground with the development of
computers and the interconnecting of PCs.

Pirates do not want the sovereign state to impose its control on cyberspace. John Perry Barlow wrote "A Declaration of the Independence of Cyberspace" as a response to the 1996 Telecommunications Act, which introduced anti-indecency measures to cyberspace that threatened freedom of speech. As Barlow put it, this new law "attempts to place more restrictive constraints on the conversation in Cyberspace than presently exist in the Senate cafeteria, where I have dined and heard colorful indecencies spoken by United States senators on every occasion I did. This bill was enacted upon us by people who haven't the slightest idea who we are or where our conversation is being conducted. It is ... as though 'the illiterate could tell you what to read.' Well, fuck them. Or, more to the point, let us now take our leave of them. They have declared war on Cyberspace. Let us show them how cunning, baffling, and powerful we can be in our own defense."[4]

The American government considered the pirate phenomenon as enough of a serious threat to launch a vast repression campaign in 1990 called a *hacker crackdown*. The Secret Service and other agencies dismantled these organizations and prosecuted them for infringing on private property in an industry that had not yet defined its standards.[5] One of the notable effects of this wave of searches and indictments was the politicization of the movement, including an emerging fringe that positioned itself in the wake of arrests as the defender of civil liberties. NGOs such as the Electronic Frontier Foundation and the Free Software Foundation gained influence and today voice many concerns of the cyberpirate organizations. In August 2011,

the pirate organization Anonymous launched a cyberattack on the San Francisco Rail Agency's website after
the Electronic Frontier Foundation criticized the agency
for restricting mobile communications on its train plat-
forms in an attempt to thwart the coordination of a protest demonstration. Often, a noteworthy consequence of
highly advertised antipiracy repression is the creation of a
rebellious image for the pirate movement, which gradually
encourages many more outsiders to join the cause.

This excerpt from a manifesto written by a member of
the Legions of the Underground gives an idea of how a
pirate organization envisions cyberspace:[6]

> *Another one got busted today*
> *Not for what you would think*
> *I nod my head in silence, yet I am crying inside*
> *Another idea stolen*
> *Another idea lost*
> *Another advance defeated*
> *...*
> *I am not like you*
> *I want to know where something comes from*
> *I want to know how something works*
> *...*
> *I give you my ideas freely*
> *You give me the Digital Millennium Copyright Act*
> *I give you information security*
> *You give me the Patriot Act*
> *...*

This madness has to stop
Information no longer wants to be free
Information IS free
. . .
You will never control what we say or think
You will never win against us all

In "A Declaration of the Independence of Cyberspace," which appears on tens of thousands of websites, the founder of the Electronic Frontier Foundation explains why state sovereignty cannot apply to digital territory:

You have no moral right to rule us nor do you possess any methods of enforcement we have true reason to fear.

Governments derive their just powers from the consent of the governed. You have neither solicited nor received ours. We did not invite you. You do not know us, nor do you know our world. Cyberspace does not lie within your borders. Do not think that you can build it, as though it were a public construction project. You cannot. It is an act of nature and it grows itself through our collective actions.

You have not engaged in our great and gathering conversation, nor did you create the wealth of our marketplaces. You do not know our culture, our ethics, or the unwritten codes that already provide our society more order than could be obtained by any of your impositions.

. . . Where there are real conflicts, where there are wrongs, we will identify them and address them by our means. We are forming our own Social Contract. This governance will arise according to the conditions of our world, not yours. Our world is different.

Clearly, the struggle between cyberpirates and the state is about which norms should govern cyberspace and who has the legitimacy to design them. This has become a global struggle, as the pirate organization in cyberspace now extends beyond the United States and Western Europe. It has proliferated into Eastern Europe, Asia, Australia, and Russia. Scott Henderson estimates that approximately 1 percent of regular Internet users are more or less linked to a pirate organization in China.[7] Some pirate groups have tens of thousands of active members and sympathizers. The Berlin-based Chaos Computer Club (CCC), founded in 1981, defines itself as "a galactic community of life forms, independent of age, sex, race or societal orientation, which strives across borders for freedom of information." As an organization, it strives "for an open, free, and neutral Internet, ... respectful of anonymity, personal data and in favor of transparency."[8] Put differently, it strives for an Internet that would be a common good administered in a decentralized fashion by its own users. An Internet that would resemble extraterritorial digital waters.

Chapter Eleven

HACKING
PROPERTY RIGHTS

*The people who call them trolls are usually large, incumbent
players that cross-license their patent portfolios with other
incumbents to form a nice, cosy oligopoly. "Trolling" is the
practice of interrupting that comfortable and predictably profitable
arrangement. It's hard to feel any sympathy for the incumbents at
all when you look at it that way.*

—Mark Shuttleworth, *Microsoft Is Not the Real Threat*, May 21, 2007

With the widespread Internet access and the emergence of
new software monopolies, originally tied to the computer
(Microsoft) and now to the user (Google), the digital territory
has become a new gray area for capitalism. We cannot say
exactly who controls or who should control the Internet or
the flow of information on the web. Should software code be
patentable, thereby preventing others from achieving similar results without citing the patent and acquiring the corresponding license? Or should code be subject to a more flexible

copyright, which allows, unlike patents, the free use of an innovative idea as long as its expression differs in form from the original material? Or, as many pirates would advocate, should code be allowed to freely circulate like the words of everyday language? These distinctions may seem subtle to the novice, but their implications are huge.

Within certain hacker communities, the electronic locks that prevent the modification of source code are seen as straitjackets imposed on users: "With the so-called digital rights management (DRM) system, the behavior of employees, consumers and citizens is being increasingly regulated by software."[1] Cyberpirates are opposed to this type of computer-code appropriation, which allows certain companies to become de facto monopolies of software applications whose licenses legally exclude the possibility of developing potentially better alternatives. In practice, software is a digital itinerary that links a problem with one of its possible solutions. In this context, licensed software forces everyone who wants to solve the same problem to take the same paying route, as, similarly, the spice merchants were required to directly pay the monopolistic company that had opened up the route to the Indies.

From the viewpoint of the pirates, code is a language that belongs to everyone, just like language or international waters: it is a common good that cannot be appropriated for any specific use. This perspective must be included in the picture along with the other viewpoints that defend the right to a legitimate return on investment and establish intellectual property devices for such an end, such as copyrights and patents.

Industrial Property: Right of Exclusion Versus Information and Public Circulation

What is a patent? A patent is granted by a sovereign state and gives its holder the right to prevent a third party from using an invention for commercial or industrial purposes. Above all, a patent is a right of exclusion. The holder can also grant licenses to use the patent. In exchange, the patent holder must list in detail the internal components so that people can understand the nature of the invention and the steps leading to this invention. Most patent laws stipulate that new inventions that are likely to be used industrially can be protected by a patent. With a patent, a private property right is granted by a sovereign for a limited period of time in a given territory in exchange for the publicity of an invention. Upon expiration, the patent lapses and becomes public domain, and all people now have the right to use freely the invention that was previously off limits to them. This accounts for the development of generic drugs after a company's exclusive usage rights expire.

Property rights vary from region to region. In Europe, the first person to file a patent holds the property right, whereas in the United States, the right goes to the person who had the idea first, known as the *first inventor*. An effective way of preventing the patentability of an innovation is to publish interim studies that show the chronology of creation. Intellectual property rights come in many different shapes and forms, from copyright, patents, and trademarks, to drawings and models. But as industrial property

has taken on increased importance over the past fifteen years, the whole concept of intellectual property has been increasingly challenged in many parts of the world.

Extending intellectual property rights goes hand in hand with extending capitalism. In the same way as some see the successive milestones accompanying the normalization of economic value in the opening up of stock markets, the creation of intellectual property agencies heralds the transformation of economic systems into a contemporary version of capitalism. This movement has led the former Eastern Bloc countries, now under European influence, to create their own patent offices under the guidance of the European Patent Office (EPO).

The advanced positions of financial capitalism continue to define new property titles (shares, bonds, copyrights, patent families, credit default swaps, etc.) and propagate sophisticated overcoding of economic value. However, at the same time, some gray areas persist. Tax havens shelter financial hackers who take advantage of the apathy of established, but sluggish, organizations—companies, banks, and even countries like Iceland or Greece. Other worldwide organizations hack brands, logos, copyrights, and patents, and sail close to the shores of illegal appropriation of surrendered value—intellectual property. In the mid-2000s, NEC Corporation was caught off guard when it discovered that another organization in East Asia had duplicated its production lines, products, and even licensing contracts with other parties.[2] French luxury brands are victims of physical and now virtual counterfeiting, with

many counterfeiters using online sales sites, such as eBay, to off-load knocked-off products. According to estimates from the target groups, the fraud rate on eBay exceeds 80 percent, and manufacturers are claiming dozens of millions of euros in damages.

How should we judge the emergence of industrial counterfeiting, illegal downloading from the Internet, and hacking of drugs developed and protected in the north by countries in the south? How much value is being ruined for holders of the property titles that have been conned? What is the net present value generated? Industrial protection allows us to value what is new—that is, what is not available currently or normally. Parties agree on a valuation of the potential benefit derived from the use of a patent, which entrusts its owner with a right to exclude others from producing certain things in the same way. The social contract underwritten by governments grants inventors this right of exclusion in exchange for public access to knowledge. But invention and innovation involve more and more complex processes and license agreements across firms, a practice known as *patent pooling*. As a consequence, the spirit of patenting has been distorted over the past decades, because the social contract between governments and inventors is increasingly mediated by private—and sometimes secret—interfirm arrangements (as illustrated by the quote at the beginning of this chapter). A common invention such as the cell phone represents a nexus of contracts involving multiple patent offices and several thousand patents held by dozens of companies.

The number of patents registered in a given year has more than doubled in the United States (going from 120,000 in 1995 to 300,000 today), as well as in Europe with the European Patent Office (from 60,000 to 150,000 during the same period). China comes first in terms of growth in the number of patent registrations and is among the top for new brand registrations. For many listed companies, most of their value stems from intangible assets, including brands, patents, and rights they license to other companies. With these renewed requests for patents, the relationship between private invention and collective well-being loosens, and the management of industrial property rights by firms becomes more offensive, blurring the line between "quality" and "quantity." So the key question is to what extent can a society accept the continuous surge of intellectual property as economically beneficial but as a right that excludes third parties from using and improving some techniques in a more open fashion.

Hacking Property Rights

With the rapid increase in value of intangible assets over the past fifteen years, some companies have acquired a large number of patents for the latent value they represent without actually producing anything. They use the patents to claim damages against established firms that have not respected industrial property rights. These patent holders can receive major compensation, especially in the United

States, where the laws favor the plaintiffs. When threat-ened with lawsuits, companies tend to pay up because if they do not, they may be banned from producing their products. These small, mobile companies that seek patents are often referred to as *trolls*, a name that is inspired by the short and aggressive beings in Scandinavian fables that lie in ambush to rob or assassinate lost travelers.[3] These modern-day trolls seek out private individuals who hold patents, or vulnerable companies that are under Chapter 11 protection, for example. They purchase these patents for next to nothing, and then they use them to attack (that is, sue) large multinational corporations.

In the "sea" of deterritorialized property rights, these trolls choose the places where norms are the most favor-able for patent holders. Partnering with lawyers who have an interest in winning their cases—a percentage of the damages never hurts—they demand that the marketing of products that infringe their patents be stopped. The sums at stake can be substantial. In 2006, the manufacturer of the BlackBerry, Research In Motion (RIM), paid $612 million in an "amicable" settlement with NTP, which holds five patents that could have blocked Research In Motion from producing BlackBerrys.

In the United States, organizations such as Acacia (which is listed on the NASDAQ), DataTreasury, Forgent, and Rembrandt Technologies are known to follow this type of strategy, yet none of them would probably agree to be labeled a pirate organization. These trolls are interested solely in the right of exclusion. They have no interest in

actually using the patent to create products. Their motives challenge our presuppositions about the capitalist innovation model and should force us to rethink the norms for property and monopolies. Trolls prevent companies from operating and they stall innovation efforts. There are benefits that certain holders of legal operating rights gain in exchange for the public disclosure of their technical processes, but trolls prevent this exchange between private protection and public knowledge to operate. Although they pretend to act in order to protect property rights and to combat oligopolies, trolls' actions seem to have a negative effect on the majority of us.

Timo Fischer and Joachim Henkel, in one of the rare academic articles on the subject, explain how the actions of these troll organizations uncover two sources of economic inefficiency.[4] First, patent offices are not always able to detect whether prior patents exist. In many cases, the offending companies have been producing goods and using technologies without knowledge of the existence of other patents. Trolls are on the lookout for these types of situations. They take advantage of these bureaucratic inefficiencies of the United States Patent and Trademark Office (USPTO) or the EPO in Europe, which are inundated with patent applications. Second, the technology market would not really work any better in the absence of trolls. In fact, instead of buying a patent or finding a holder who would be willing to grant a user license, impatient manufacturing firms tend to reinvent what already exists, even if it means they will be confronted by trolls.

These established firms focus a lot of energy to invalidate practices of the trolls, on the grounds that trolls disrespect both the spirit and the letter of the patents. In other words, trolls move the whole patenting system away from its original function. Trolls are not looking to use patents for their productive and innovative virtues. They are and will remain nonproductive owners—a parasite in the system. In return, trolls condemn the established firms as oligarchies because they use cross license agreements for their patents. The trolls defend themselves by pointing to other organizations that do not actually manufacture products from their own discoveries and intellectual property rights. One example is university laboratories, whose mission is research and its application, not production. Also, state legislation allows university labs to provide, through agreements, the transfer of property rights to established firms. As trolls point out, why would this behavior be acceptable for labs and organizations of the milieu but unacceptable for those operating from the fringes?

This is a thorny issue. Who are the real defenders of competition and economic freedom? Is it the pirate organization that uses ownership rights on industrial property without actually producing anything? Established firms that sign nontransparent cross licensing agreements, exchange patents between themselves for a royalty, yet offer in return sophisticated products used by a large number of people? How can the real territory be defined for establishing the right of exclusion that a patent represents? Should we accept that ownership be universally defined as being

both the possession and the utilization of a property right, or could the two be decoupled, depending on the location? Which side should states take in this growing gray area in which pirate organizations attack legal and legitimate companies, as they navigate through various territories, each with its own set of norms?

Recent cases in the United States show that the law is less likely to bend in favor of trolls. Since the *MedImmune v. Genentech* case in 2007, trolls must demonstrate that the company under attack had "reckless disregard" for the rights of the patent holder, whereas in the past the offending company had the duty to take the patent holder's rights into account. In addition, the quality of the patent must be proved in order for the case to go forward. In the *KSR v. Teleflex* case, the Supreme Court gave reason to KSR, which argued that the combination between two subcomponents was "obvious" and could not be patented—and therefore did not infringe on the rights of Teleflex, the plaintiff. Since then, the USPTO has circulated an internal memorandum to justify its reversal decisions based on an understanding of "why a person of ordinary skill in the art would have combined the prior art elements in the manner claimed." From now on, ownership of patents that contain a combination of elements familiar to the scientific community does not constitute enough substance for plaintiffs. Omitting to refer to such a patent by an established firm can no longer be held against it by the plaintiffs, hence limiting the trolls' pretentions.

What matters is the long-term change brought about by pirate organizations and the variations they introduce to the heart of capitalist code. Pirates claim a right to expand or redefine the concept of property, and they challenge monopolies or unfair oligopolies. They force states to take into account the public cause as they rethink business norms to avoid the exclusion of even more economic actors, which would push them aside further to the fringes and turn them into pirates. Norms of exchange and competition are thus constantly redefined as the sovereign decides to keep in or out elements of the public cause defended and embodied by pirate organizations.

IS THE PIRATE ORGANIZATION A FAIR COMPETITOR?

Agreements and cartels, because they protect against the destructive impact of financial concentrations, allow small and medium-sized businesses to survive. Now, it is because of these small and medium-sized businesses that economic and social relationships remain reasonable and avoid becoming unbearable and inhuman.

—Auguste Detoeuf, CEO of Alsthom, 1938

An industry that has to suspend civil liberties to make money is an industry the world needs to be without.

—Ryan Moffitt, founder of the Florida Pirate Party

Each capitalist revolution brings about its local and contextual opposition. Today, cyberpirates defend the right to access and reproduce digital files freely. Trolls claim the right to property regardless of whether that property is used in practice. Just as capitalism expands into partially uncharted territories in multiple ways, so do pirate

organizations that use a large variety of tactics to decode the norms of capitalism.

Normal Capitalism and Free Competition

There is a Darwinian vision of capitalism that claims the best and most powerful organizations will always prevail. According to this "ecological" perspective, the selection constraints on competing firms apply uniformly to each of them.[1] Instead of a specific firm being retained, the pressures of competition and legitimacy eliminate entire populations of firms.

Let's think about agricultural cooperatives, credit union banks, or independent gas stations. Each of these populations of firms, akin to species in biology, has specific features: a distinct capital ownership, specific relationships with suppliers or clients, and its own rules for the management of resources and the allocation of investments and profits. Competition opposes rival populations rather than particular firms. The agricultural co-op system is challenged by profit-seeking agrochemical companies. Credit union banks must regroup to face the pressure from new global bankers. Independent gas stations offering a single service cannot compete with the twenty-four-hour superstores for which gas is but one of the many products offered to customers.

Another illustration of this phenomenon can be found in the history of the East India Companies. For more than two centuries, they prospered in Europe, but then they

gradually disappeared within a period of fifty years, until they ceased to exist in 1858. Stable establishment of trading posts and military bases in the nineteenth century around the world progressively made the use of the "Indies companies" obsolete, as well as the reliance on hired mercenaries and corsairs. Permanent establishments, which soon became territorial colonies, replaced the temporary bases upon which modern-age international trade had relied.

The international convention of Paris in 1856 heralded a new conception of maritime territory, which was henceforth recognized by the main powers as *res omnium communis*, or "property as a common heritage of all mankind" (the proximity in time between the death of the last East India company and the signing of the Paris convention is telling). This new norm favored the strongest states that had the largest number of trained troops and the securest trading posts. But it also allowed everyone to freely navigate the seas without piratical threats as long as they remained in international waters (which now account for more than 50 percent of all navigable water surfaces).

In a similar fashion, it is the advent of new normative features that explains the growth and decline of troll organizations. At the turn of the twenty-first century, the strengthening of industrial property rights enforcement, orchestrated by the state, facilitated the emergence and increased the viability of troll organizations. In turn, from 2007 onward, new norms have emerged as a response to the troll threat, and the renewed guidelines for industrial property rights protection have forced trolls to retreat.

According to this Darwinian vision of economic selection, the most legitimate and most resistant form survives. Comparatively, organizations of the milieu spawn more and die out less often than pirate organizations do. So, despite its historical permanence, the pirate organization is less resistant to established economic and legal pressures than legitimate organizations. Yet, in partially uncharted territories, pirate organizations can benefit from an advantage they hold over legitimate organizations. They are mobile, their rivals not yet established lack credibility and resources, and they can voice their public cause loud enough to influence the writing of the capitalistic code. Because the normalization process continually extends itself, the pirate organization constantly decodes the sovereign's maneuvers and subsequently adjusts its claims based on the current conditions within the gray areas of capitalism.

Forms of Competition and the Selection of Organizations

In light of this Darwin-inspired analysis, competition is a natural force, which, like natural selection, eliminates the weakest and less able, and keeps only the fittest competitors. This ecological analysis definitely helps clarify concrete realities; for example, why the East India Companies, which generated annual profit rates around 30 percent throughout the seventeenth century, easily outlasted independent buccaneers, who for the most part struggled for survival. However,

Darwinian models of competition are relatively nearsighted when it comes to explaining large capitalist movements or the recurrent motif of pirate contestation from era to era, since they assume that the major waves of normalization are exogenous to economic phenomena.

We hope to propose an alternative vision. The historical and institutional context is essential in understanding why profit is seen as legitimate and when it is acceptable or not to dismantle organizations (the Indies companies, the BBC, Microsoft, or Anonymous). The free market version of competition inspired by neo-Darwinian interpretations serves as a point of departure for reflection. It is in no way a finishing point, just a theoretical draft, an extreme case that rarely materializes. The state never ceases to intervene, to overcode, to separate the precisely viable from that which can disappear, to declare what is legitimate profit and what is bankruptcy. Digging its claws into partially uncharted territories, the sovereign state maps out the conditions for competition, which varies from place to place and time to time. During this process of normalization, some organizations of the milieu seek to impose their views, to protect their assets, and to expand their influence. For instance, the first epigraph at the beginning of the chapter illustrates the ideological conflicts that occurred in the circles defining industrial policy in France during the 1930s, opposing free market advocates and proponents of controlled economic expansion. Detoeuf is a typical representative of the latter movement. Before the war, he acted as the CEO of Alsthom, a huge industrial conglomerate, and as the

vice president of the commission establishing the French accounting plan during the war. He wrote the famous speech on the end of free market economics in 1936, when he promoted an organized economy, wishing to define a protective "neo-capitalism" for small and medium-size firms that would shield them from free-for-all competition.

Let's look at another example. At the end of the Civil War, the economic conditions in the United States had seriously deteriorated. Yet during this bleak period, a generation of fearless entrepreneurs built industrial and financial empires. These figureheads of American capitalism remain in our memory: J. P. Morgan, Andrew Carnegie, and John D. Rockefeller. But after a few decades, the hegemonic empires created by these famous men were disputed by those workers who helped expand to the West, dug oil wells, laid railway tracks, and blasted mountains, looking for ores and gems. Farmers united, craftsmen came together in lobbies, and unions channeled people's discontentment in the face of economic opulence. These rich entrepreneurs wanted to redefine the rules of competition, as sustaining success in this new territory was tenuous at best. Around 1880, more and more collusive behaviors appeared in order to stabilize the economic environment. Cartels and other agreements spread to the point where prices of commodities (iron, oil, coal, and so forth) and services (distribution, transportation) were fixed by private firms in a way that guaranteed them hefty profits that could not be competed away. In 1890, a famous law, the Sherman Antitrust Act, was enacted with the goal of eliminating such agreements.

The Sherman Act declared cartels illegal in order to protect fair competition between rival companies. However, collaboration and mergers between companies was legal within each state. During this time, New Jersey became the first state to authorize the creation of legal structures whose mission was to hold shares in companies. From this, holding companies were born. Ironically, although cartels between states were effectively being fought against (more than three hundred sensational court cases within a span of 30 years), the anticartel law was also the starting point for a wave of mergers and holding company development. This, in another way, jump-started a process that ended instituting many local or national oligopolies.[2] This example illustrates the way in which the rules of competition are occasionally redefined, and include or reject organizations from within the changing milieu. Some of the excluded organizations can be or become "pirate" and contest the validity of just-born norms.

Accordingly, some sociologists have shown that organization of firms and markets is affected by not only national history but also local context. Thus, in the United States, federal law encouraged from the start the fixing of prices between competing investors in the railway business by declaring the industry to be "naturally cooperative."[3] According to Amasa Stone, a pioneer in the American railway industry, "the time ha[d] come when the possession of railroad lines [wa]s useless without a total cooperation between rival lines."[4] However, after the Sherman Act, which banned these agreements between states, rate competition became all the rage, and mergers and acquisitions were encouraged

by bankers who feared an erosion of the value of the assets they helped finance. Specialists in railway economy then qualified the industry as "naturally monopolistic" to justify these repurchases and the effective domination of a single operator per main line—a system that finally consisted of the juxtaposition of regional monopolies that nevertheless maintained the illusion of competition at the national level.

During this same period, AT&T began to expand into a monopoly as the normalization of the analog space of communications was under way. AT&T had made itself an indispensable service provider even before Bell's telephony patent expired in 1894. By the time competitors could enter the telephony market, AT&T had used its monopoly rents to subsidize the construction of a national network. Armed with the largest customer base, AT&T kept attracting more new subscribers than any other competitor, owing to interoperability problems across competing networks (i.e., new subscribers had incentives to sign up with the company allowing them to reach the largest number of people across the United States). In a bold lobbying effort, AT&T pushed forward the idea that telephony was a "natural monopoly" by arguing that duplicating phone lines between, say, New York City and Chicago was a waste of capital, since it amounted to investing in redundant infrastructure. Competitors had to share the network of the organization that had first laid out the infrastructure, in exchange for a fee. Because of AT&T's initial advantage and huge cash reserves, it was virtually impossible for competitors to gain market share. AT&T further reinforced its unfair

advantage by imposing the use of AT&T-approved tele-
phones that were leased to customers for a monthly fee
and by managing a network of loosely connected subsidiaries that operated localized monopolies within an over-
all corporate structure designed to exploit every loophole
in current antitrust law. Invoking the Sherman Act, the
American government threatened to nationalize AT&T.
But the company once again succeeded in convincing the
government that the competitive situation in the telephone
industry was a natural monopoly.

To circumvent the Sherman Act, AT&T adopted a
strategy to sign local agreements with companies that had
a stronghold in a given geographic area. This strategy
allowed AT&T to work its way to the top of a lucrative
cartel of price fixing. Before long, AT&T's methods were
challenged by thousands of telephone pirates, or "phone
phreaks." These pirates, whose history has been partially
documented in Bruce Sterling's work, *The Hacker Crackdown*, developed a series of techniques that allowed them to
use AT&T lines free of charge without being caught.[5] Post-
WWII, one of the most popular tactics among the pirates
was to use a *blue box*. This simple electronic device reproduced a sound of the same frequency used by AT&T—
2600 hertz—which enabled users to connect to the AT&T
network. Steve Jobs and Steve Wozniak, the two cofound-
ers of Apple, had built up a reputation as rebels on Califor-
nia campuses by selling blue boxes to a number of students
who wanted to make free phone calls. The phone phreaks
of the 1970s did not understand the illegitimacy of using

the network without paying. In their minds, their wrong-doing did not cost anyone anything and did not exclude new users from benefiting from the same service. Another act of piracy involved the attack of telephone booths by increasingly inventive phreaks who circumvented the mechanism that connects the machine's coin-operated device with the telephone network. In the New York area, more than 150,000 cases of pirated telephone booths were reported annually.

The normalization of business and economic activity does not result from the natural laws of economic selection. It is the result of collective enactments of principles that define competition and establish what legitimate profits are. The pirate organization, sometimes under the guise of a robber baron, participates in this enactment process by contesting the privileges of past or present monopolies. From 1870 to 1970, the economic history of the United States showed that business leaders took possession of partially uncharted territories and codefined the norms of competition. Taking land and mines, the mountains and their resources, and tiptoeing around ever-changing laws, these leaders shaped the development of the West. For their part, pirate organizations were foiled in their attempts to denounce the new norms that tried to reset the rules of "fair" competition and redefine what legitimate profits or bankruptcy were (e.g., the Sherman Act or, more recently, the Telecommunications Act of 1995). While it seems that the pirate organization is an ever-failing condition, pirates do manage to imprint the future trajectories of capitalism.

THE PIRATE
ORGANIZATION
AND THE BUILDING
BLOCKS OF LIFE

Life is basically the result of an information process, a software process. We have created the first species that has a computer for a mother, and that is capable of reproducing, on this planet.

—Craig Venter, founder of Celera Genomics, 2010

When we think of territories, we tend to think of land masses. By this measure, the territorial expansion and normalization process that began in 1492 came to an end in 1899, when an international conference came to the conclusion that every emerged territory on Earth had a sovereign owner. But this isn't right, is it? As physicist Richard Feynman said, "There is plenty of room at the bottom"—in this instance, at the micro- and nanoscopic scales. And that space represents partially uncharted territory. The

discovery of DNA in 1953 heralded the beginning of a new topographical era, only fifty-four years removed from the date the last land mass found an owner. In 2000, Tony Blair and Bill Clinton announced that the "first complete map" of the human genome had just been established by an international public consortium, the Human Genome Project, as the result of an unprecedented cooperative effort. At the time, this exploit was compared with the first voyage to the Moon and the first map of American territory unrolled by Thomas Jefferson.[1] Back then, the genome map did not yet fall under the territory of capitalism, but it didn't take long for the normalization process to begin.

Biocorsair and Biopirate Organizations: The Venter Case

Craig Venter's exploits date back to the beginning of the 1990s. At the time, he decided to register patents on the genes whose sequencing he was overseeing at the National Institutes of Health (NIH), a government-funded organization. Venter's attempt caused a scandal, since he was attempting to appropriate the living. Taking advantage of the vagueness of biogenetic regulations, Venter left the NIH and founded a private organization called Celera Genomics in 1998. Venter's aim was to compete with the Human Genome Project in the race to fully sequence human DNA. The bet paid off: despite starting eight years behind, Celera crossed the finish line at the same time as the Human Genome Project. Venter

announced in 2000 that Celera Genomics had produced a complete genetic map of a human being.

Celera's methods for decrypting DNA were less refined than those used by the Human Genome Project. Mainly computational, they used electronic sequencers with massive processing power. Celera was funded by private investors who expected returns on the patenting of discoveries stemming from the intermediary decoding of the genome. To make up for lost time, Celera also integrated into its genome map the results published and made freely available by the Human Genome Project as they became available. Venter took seriously the words of the cyberpirate Digital Ebola—in order to "hack the machine, you must first hack yourself"—offering Celera his own DNA as a target for the first "hacking" of the human genome outside of any direct sovereign control.[2] His own genome thus became the template for the first map of a new gray area in capitalist expansion.

Clonaid and Celera are two notorious pirate organizations that operate in biogenetic territory. They are not alone, and it is not their intention of leaving things at that. In 2002, Venter left Celera to create the Craig Venter Institute (CVI), whose objective is to create a synthetic form of life. Unlike the dubious doctors who worked for Raël, the group that had human cloning high on its agenda, CVI researchers met the stringent standards of scientific and academic rigor. In 2007, CVI developed *mycoplasma laboratorium*, the first synthetic chromosome ever created in a laboratory. In 2010, very special bacteria came out of

CVI's laboratories: its entire DNA stemmed from a chemical synthesis generated by machines conceived by Venter's team. According to researchers, this spectacular advance opened the door to the artificial creation of new living species ("synthetic life"). In order to have their discovery validated by the editors of the prestigious journal *Science*, CVI biologists had to prove the synthetic character of the bacteria's DNA by incorporating into it a coded text that would guarantee the artificial origin of the macromolecule. Venter chose to include several excerpts in this encrypted text, including another famous Feynman quote: "What I cannot rebuild, I cannot understand."

This quotation could become the calling card for an entire generation of biopirates who manipulate DNA in makeshift laboratories, often for the fun of it, but sometimes also because they dream of a world in which each citizen would be responsible for the management and improvement of his own biological capital (organs, stem cells, etc.). Contrary to conventional wisdom, it is not necessary to have an extensive education or major financial means to tinker with DNA, say, in one's garage. The processing power of personal computers will soon be sufficient for sequencing a DNA molecule at home. Also, the costs of acquiring this knowledge and the instruments required to modify or recombine a DNA molecule decrease by the month. Today, these underground practices pose little risk of catastrophe. We don't have to worry about deadly viruses. But tomorrow, who knows? Various multinational reports point to this as a real threat, which will only loom

larger in the years to come.[3] Markus Schmidt, an expert in biosecurity, called on authorities to debate this issue now, because in a few years, "it will be too late to go back and close this Pandora's box."[4] The "DIYbio" movement, which brings together dozens of independent laboratories worldwide, plans to make all biological engineering available to everyone so that control of the biogenetic space will no longer be the monopoly of state-sponsored research institutes.

Legitimately Expropriating Humanity?

In biogenetic territory, organizations of the milieu seek patents, a goal that goes against a basic principle of piracy. As we've mentioned previously, the pirate organization fights against state-granted privileges in the name of a different cause (e.g., putting forth a more equal sharing), but organizations of the milieu like Monsanto seem to take away what belongs to everyone. They do so presumably to improve on nature and adapt each crop or animal to local conditions—climatic or feeding, for instance. By genetically modifying the DNA of a plant species and then patenting it, these organizations can lay claim to the ownership of this species. Then they can decide whether or not to impose the payment of royalties on the users who have been supplied with seeds. As a consequence, growing methods that have been used throughout the ages for certain plant species are now infringing on a property right that did not exist before. For

many opponents, companies who pursue these patenting practices are expropriating humanity and privatizing what should otherwise benefit society as a whole.

By law, a species whose genotype has been patented can only be cultivated where the organization holding the patent authorizes it. TRIPS agreements (Agreement on Trade-Related Aspects of Intellectual Property Rights) promoted by the World Trade Organization set down minimum standards for intellectual property rights. They recognize the ability to patent life that has been modified in the laboratory, but not life modified on farms, as specialists consider these changes unstable. If such a norm were to be imposed on everyone, legitimate organizations would gain a tremendous advantage in exploiting the living. A rival norm, defended by the UN, the Convention of Biodiversity (CBD), proposes as an alternative the transfer of responsibility for the gene pool to sovereign states. This solution would favor state organizations such as the NIH as well as the subcontracting of borderline research to biocorsair organizations. In any case, the normative indeterminacy surrounding ownership of the living is now at its peak. While about 20 percent of the human genome is already targeted by one or more of forty thousand US patents, a recent US court ruling took a first step in invalidating DNA patenting as a whole on the grounds that genes are part of nature and thus a common heritage. In a brief issued by the Department of Justice, it is acknowledged that "this conclusion is contrary to the longstanding practice of the Patent and Trademark Office, as well as the practice of the

National Institutes of Health and other government agencies that have in the past sought and obtained patents for isolated genomic DNA."[5]

This ongoing debate is reminiscent of a time when the pirates of the seas disputed the monopolies of the Indies companies and fought the state's corsairs. However, the oceans no longer constitute the preferred space for capitalist deterritorialization. With respect to maritime routes, norms have developed since the second half of the nineteenth century and have stabilized today around the principle of "the common heritage of humanity," which, on the high seas, excluded both private appropriation and sovereign expropriation.[6] These principles as yet do not apply to the gray area of DNA. Biogenetic territory is still partially uncharted.

Ultimate Consequences: The Evolution of Life and Capitalist Evolution

Daniel Heller-Roazen traced a genealogy of pirates that goes from the common enemy of all (*communis hostis omnium*, as described by Cicero) to the enemy of humanity (*hostis humani generis*).[7] At the same time *humanity* was becoming the central character in history, from the sixteenth century onward, states began to normalize the entire globe and to acknowledge the finite nature of our world. As far as territorial expansion is concerned, capitalism is done with the surface of the Earth. Thus, nowadays,

the opening up of new spaces is only possible in infravisible limbo or outer space: biopiracy, nanopiracy, and space piracy are arising or will arise. As with so many organizations before, their acts deemed illegal under the accepted principles of their era will reshape the very territoriality of these invisible worlds and contribute to promulgating codes suited to take the capitalist machine to the next level.

While pirate and corsair organizations have always produced technological, social, and political mutations by diffusing alternative norms, the biogenetic territory presents a substantially different situation than what played out on the high seas, airwaves, or the Internet. Designing norms for DNA manipulation is not just mapping out the biogenetic territory, but also setting new boundaries on the nature of life itself. For this reason, and for the first time in history, the evolution of capitalism and the evolution of living species could literally begin to intertwine. This potentially explosive junction could reverse a great number of standards that we take for granted, and the normalization of the living could profoundly change mankind's relation to other territories.

Throughout the twentieth century, biopolitics as defined by Michel Foucault reigned supreme. The state's role was to normalize territories so as to make them suitable for its citizens. But what will happen when individuals and organizations are able to modify genetic code and hybridize living species? Instead of modeling social norms to adjust the territory to the species with which it is populated, organizations would be able to opt for a more direct intervention on

the species' biological features, provided that they remain owners of the living thus remodeled (e.g., by claiming patenting rights on modified DNA). This would undoubtedly upset the nature of capitalism much more than, say, the creation of a Tobin tax or a Zapatista revolution in Chiapas. The consequence of such an upheaval would be threefold.

First, because efforts aimed at conquering DNA or space typically involve transnational teams and funding, the deterritorialization of both human life and space would have to occur within a world system based on a principle of sovereignty expanded to the supranational level. The norms applicable to biogenetic and extraterrestrial territories would need to be defined at a high level that would go above and beyond the particular interests of any given nation-state. Although the multinational Human Genome Project represented a move in this direction, the ongoing space race still puts nation-states in direct competition. In particular, the Chinese plan to return to the Moon seriously calls into question the normalization of the Moon's surface and underground "on behalf of humanity."

Second, the increasing contribution of private capital to such expansion efforts strengthens the position of organizations of the milicu, but it also strengthens those on the fringes, both pirate and corsair. The normalization of exchanges as implemented by new coalitions involving multiple states and organizations is therefore embarking on a new phase for which the definitions of property, responsibility, and legitimate profit are still in the works. Organizations such as Celera are competing directly with

the sovereign states regarding technological breakthroughs. With every advance, they are questioning the current capitalistic code of property. They contribute to normalizing the gray areas, fighting fiercely for their cause as pirates or accepting a letter of marque from the sovereign to continue their research as corsairs. Today, the terms and conditions for the codes concerning legitimate property are waiting to be defined—or codefined by these new coalitions.

Moreover, to achieve its expansion over the partially uncharted biogenetic and extraterrestrial territories, the state must normalize increasingly specialized and delocalized competences to successfully maintain its control and prevent temporary social structures from being established to its detriment—and to the detriment of the societies from which it stems. The problem here is that the ideals upon which the nation-state system has been premised over the last centuries may not fit the needs of such ambitious expansion plans. On whose behalf can the Human Genome Project or a multinational mission to the Moon be implemented, and with what official purpose? Because the will of "the people" can only be expressed within the current geopolitical system at the nation-state level, and typically in the name of democracy, who is to validate future expansion plans designed beyond the traditional boundaries of the Westphalian sovereign state? If governments cannot resolve this dilemma anytime soon, pirate organizations may just end up preempting the territories that sovereigns are leaving behind because of their inability to update the now archaic nation-state system.

Pirate organizations seem to be more ready than most states to switch their attention to the transnational level. WikiLeaks and Anonymous, just like the sea pirates of the seventeenth century, claim to serve a purpose that goes beyond the idiosyncratic needs and wishes of any particular sovereign state. In fact, pirate organizations have almost always operated above and beyond the boundaries of the Westphalian nation-state system. From an evolutionary perspective, they may well enjoy a competitive edge over the sovereigns as normalization becomes essentially a transnational process.

Finally, this puts into question the symbiotic relationship between the state and capitalism. Powerful organizations of the milieu—Google and Amazon in cyberspace, CVI and Monsanto in biogenetic territory—and probably pirate organizations from the fringes as well represent the most powerful driver of change, as global capitalism ceases to be a sovereign-centric network and morphs into something else.

THE FUTURE OF THE
CAPITALIST STATE

*The history of mankind can be seen, in the large, as the realization
of Nature's secret plan to bring forth a perfectly constituted state as
the only condition in which the capacities of mankind can be fully
developed, and also bring forth that external relation among states
which is perfectly adequate to this end.*

—Immanuel Kant, "Idea for a Universal History with a Cosmopolitan
Purpose," 8th Proposal, 1784

The sovereign state for nearly four centuries fought against
the pirate organization, which contested territorial expansion and the normalization of trade. Today, sovereign
states are caught between the pirate organization and a
series of metasovereign organizations with wide-reaching
normative capabilities, impressive overcoding power, and
a reservoir of monetary and human capital.

The idea of sovereignty is in the process of changing as
the number of multinational organizations grows. Some

are politico-legal, like the UN or the European Union, which extend their influence to an ever-increasing number of areas and seek the emergence of regional and international metasovereignties. Others are economic, such as financial markets that trade more and more assets and increasingly sophisticated derivatives. Others, such as banks, insurance companies, and hedge funds, impinge on state sovereignty by using the debt of struggling companies and governments as their currency. The bankruptcy of Iceland and Greece (and possibly Spain and Portugal) and the attempt at a resolution for the euro monetary crisis through the involvement of private debt holders illustrate this new landscape.

In this turbulent era, certain states have already chosen their camp. The Bahamian archipelago, as part of a de facto alliance with the pirate organization, is host to, for example, Clonaid-style semiclandestine laboratories, money-laundering establishments, "sensitive" computer servers, and so forth. Iceland has overtly teamed up with WikiLeaks to design a series of thirteen laws under the Iceland Modern Media Initiative, whose goal is to turn Iceland into a haven for the freedom of speech, expression, and information. This partnership between the state and the pirate organization began soon after an Icelandic news channel was pressured into not covering the publication of a local bank's loan book, which was obtained by WikiLeaks. Other states are seeking to attract the finance world in order to accelerate economic deterritorialization and dematerialization rather than being subjected to it. Yet

others, such as the member states of the Eurogroup, come together in a metasovereign structure—which gives rise to a whole range of institutional problems in the event of a financial crisis like the one Greece has had to go through since 2010. Instead of public debt crises, the total independence claimed by certain organizations is the greatest risk facing the sovereign state and its four-century-long marriage with capitalism.

Sealand: A Pirate Sovereignty?

As early as 1966, a former British soldier turned pirate radio DJ decided to challenge the limits of sovereignty. He took possession of a fort that had been abandoned after the Second World War in international waters, off the English coast. Skillfully exploiting the noble idea of the right of nations to self-determination, he renamed the fort Sealand and declared its independence. Then he started calling himself Prince Roy and made his intention clear: "Sealand was founded on the principle that any group of people dissatisfied with the oppressive laws and restrictions of existing nation states may declare independence in any place not claimed to be under the jurisdiction of another sovereign entity."[1]

Prince Roy quickly created a state company that oversaw all Sealand affairs: the issuing of passports, granting of visas, printing of bank notes in Sealand currency, and development of the local economy. Regarding this last

point, business is going rather well. Sealand attracts all sorts of businesspeople who are looking to conceal activities that are considered illegal in other parts of the world. HavenCo developed discreet hosting activities in Sealand for computer servers storing illicit content, especially content associated with online gambling, tax evasion, or sharing copyrighted files. For about forty euros, anyone can become a citizen of Sealand and receive official documents that are issued by the Sealand administration. Newcomers can choose between two noble titles: lord or baron. For an additional twenty euros, you can become a premium citizen and receive a citizenship title autographed by Prince Roy himself. Sealand is a libertarian sovereign state that sells its privileges and segments the citizenship market.

The State versus the Pirate Organization: What Vessel for Capitalistic Expansion?

The extreme case of Sealand raises a simple question: can sovereignty one day become the subject of capitalist deterritorialization? After all, peasants left their native soil to work in factories, and the feudal system yielded to the central state. Massive shifts have happened in the past and more are to be expected. Could capitalism unfold within a radically different system—one that would not be centered around the nation-state? Could non–state organizations grant some form of citizenship to individuals? Being

prouder of one's company than of one's country? Defining one's identity as a member of an organization before being Greek or American or British? Even if nationality does not officially have a price, everyone knows that certain stolen passports are worth more than others on the black market. This is also true of sovereign territory. Conquering, mapping, and normalizing territory is a long, difficult, and costly process for the state. So why not sell or lease parts of it to a separatist movement or value-creating organization in order to recoup the cost—why not make sovereign territory a tradable good?

It may sound crazy now, but these types of transactions happened in the past. Islands in the East Indies were sometimes purchased or exchanged between European sovereigns. In 1674, the Dutch gave away Manhattan Island to the English as part of the Treaty of Westminster, in exchange for the guarantee that Suriname would remain Dutch. The British South Africa Company, established in 1889 by Cecil Rhodes, had the same prerogatives as a sovereign state over the British colony named Rhodesia. The company was authorized to sign treaties with neighboring powers, to own and trade land, and to maintain an army and a police force.

Early in 2010, for unclear reasons, Kazakhstan signed an agreement to lease nearly a million hectares of its territory to China. Opponents denounced the lease as a violation of the country's sovereignty, taking their discontentment to the streets and carrying signs reading THE DESTINY OF THE LAND IS THE DESTINY OF THE NATION and KAZAKH LAND IS OUR LAND.

The Kazakh president pretended not to understand what could possibly be wrong with his move—really, why shouldn't he lease this unproductive piece of land to businesspeople willing to pay a high rent for it?

It is not hard to imagine ways in which capitalism could become increasingly independent from the sovereign state. Capitalism could seek out a coupling with other semistable organizational forms to pursue new territories, to assemble flows of capital and labor in new ways, or to normalize new trading activities. Portions of sovereign territories could also be deterritorialized and connected to flows of resources held by private organizations, leading to the creation of "franchises" within the sovereign state. Which organizations would be in the best position to overcode the flows currently controlled by the state? Would it be organizations of the milieu, which influence norms of exchange in order to achieve a symbiosis with the state divested of its prerogatives? Or pirate organizations, which would move from the fringes to the inside of known territories to spread the pirate code? Put simply, who should we trust more to defend our rights as "netizens"? Homeland Security, Google, or Anonymous?

Answering these questions is far from easy. Immanuel Kant believed that there could be harmony among the sovereign states, as stated in the epigraph at the beginning of the chapter. Yet, the state form itself is not a steadfast and immutable entity. What about the pirate organization? Even though it does not assert itself in the long term as an alternative to the sovereign state, the pirate organization

does successfully participate in the development of capitalism. What does this mean? Historically, the pirate organization spreads certain normative patterns that are replicated and incorporated into capitalism, either as alterations or in their original form. In the end, these variations change the structure of capitalism in a largely unforeseeable way. By bringing about mutations in the sovereign code, the pirate organization modifies the direction of capitalism's future.

Again and again, capitalism joins together deterritorialized flows. It recombines and transforms what currently exists. There is a sharp distinction, however, between current pirate organizations and the pirate organizations of yore. The latter did not fundamentally modify the substratum of flows being combined and recombined. Today's and tomorrow's pirate and corsair organizations have the potential to make such changes. As they tinker with DNA, biopirates could alter the very abilities of human beings, not only in their physical dimension but also at a cognitive level. This will force us, in the future, to clearly define what we mean by *humanity* if we want that notion to remain the referent for determining the legitimacy of territorial control. Today's pirates can force sovereigns to withdraw unwanted bills such as the Stop Online Privacy Act (SOPA) or the Anti-Counterfeiting Trade Agreement (ACTA), rejected by a large majority at the European Parliament in July 2012, following waves of street protest in various European countries. Maybe more than ever, pirate organizations have the power to alter the capitalistic code. *They* are legions.

The crucial question is whether capitalism itself has a transcendental limit to its own progression, to exploiting resources and combining deterritorialized flows. Indeed, nothing guarantees that the sovereign state will indefinitely maintain its stranglehold over capitalist expansion, the conquest of new territories, and the normalization of flows. Can organizations of the milieu be a vector of transnational changes and a new vehicle of capitalist expansion? Can other powerful organizations from the fringes, such as the pirate organization, bring the public cause of humanity to a higher level than the sovereign state can?

Chapter Fifteen

CONCLUSION:
To the Fringes and Back

One of the ironies about modern situations is that we would have to retroactively prohibit everything that we risked to make them happen.

—Sloterdijk, *Crystal Palace*

In the capitalistic system, the states and firms operate in their respective territories by establishing codes that exclude a certain number of renegades who come together within the pirate organization. Courted and feared by states and organizations of the milieu alike, the pirate organization breaks the existing codes and creates new ones, which will later be reappropriated by legitimate governments and organizations. This explains why the Pentagon and Microsoft track hackers in cyberspace to offer them a job or why pirate Francis Drake became a corsair before being knighted by the Queen of England. Because of its sociopolitical makeup, the pirate organization has the

best chance at changing the conventions of the time and at upsetting the structure of capitalism—for example, by accepting women for the first time as sailors on ships in the seventeenth century or by modifying copyrighted material.

The pirate phenomenon began at the advent of the sovereign state and continues with the rise of globalism. Pirates are off-limits, on the fringes of territories, cities, or states. They make use of the legal conflicts between states, at times attacked by them and at other times protected by them. The pirate organization blurs the lines by reshaping the normative agenda carried out by the sovereign state. In the era of the great discoveries, when the state expanded its geographical reach, the pirate organization challenged the codes that were being imposed on the new territories of capitalism. This struggle to define the norm has haunted the history of capitalist societies and has played out in different ages and territories.

The pirate organization outpaces our attempts at categorization. Are pirates simple bandits or counterfeiters? Enemies of humanity? Defenders of a public cause? Agents of capitalist normalization? Oftentimes, they are all of those things together. We must correct the vision of capitalism as a simple accelerator of economic transactions, which becomes uncontrollable, sagging under the growing weight of its own mass that transforms everything into an endlessly reconvertible unit of capital. We need to understand the relationship between the pirate organization and capitalism, both of which are inseparable from the sovereign state.

For many analysts of the current crisis, on the one hand there are the mechanisms that generate profit but become unstable without regulation, and on the other hand there are the social struggles that allow us to balance welfare distribution. Subprimes versus Occupy Wall Street. By switching perspectives, we can see that the pirate organization reveals the essence of cyclic capitalist crises. The pirate organization enables states and organizations of the milieu to redefine territories that are suitable for competition and to normalize exchange between parties. In a certain way, the archetype of the capitalist crisis is not so much a stock market crash as it is the geopolitical struggle forced upon the state by the pirate organization, which imposes a new pairing between partially uncharted territories and their normative fabric in the making.

The pirate organization is a counterpart to capitalism that shifts norms and redraws the boundaries imposed by the sovereign. Normalizing a territory means expanding the set spaces on which a code can be practiced, deterritorialized resources can be assembled, and flows of men, products, and capital can be circulated. However, moving into gray areas also contributes to the rapid development of the pirate organization, which in turn slows the advancement of the sovereign. Therefore, the pirate organization has the opportunity to overstep the boundaries and decide for itself whether or not goods should be exchanged or stolen. The pirate organization confronts organizations of the milieu in a partially uncharted territory that the state claims to be in control of, and wherein it defines property rights, monopoly, and profit. Moving away

from a vision of capitalism in which money constantly privatizes the public domain, swallows it, and expands its reign, this essay conceives of the pirate organization as a provocative element that shifts the trajectory of capitalism.

Some see capitalist evolution as being based on decontextualized "laws of nature" (e.g., the fittest always survive as human societies move inevitably toward greater economic efficacy). Others conceive of societies as organizationless—they see heroic individuals, such as entrepreneurs, activists, or political leaders, as the only true force that can change the world. Some still believe in the pipe dream of united social classes bound to actualize a destiny that has already been written. By choosing to examine the intermediate level of the organization, we are hopeful that this analysis appears more realistic and perhaps sturdier. For example, the Dutch East India Company, year after year, accrued abysmal financial losses for decades before disappearing. Does the law of natural economic selection apply to its case? Not really. Was it "too big to fail," as some current financial institutions have been said to be? What does the catchphrase *too big to fail* conceal? That principles of competition are not natural but contingent upon a struggle between sovereign states, organizations of the milieu, and pirate organizations.

We have also tried to avoid other simplifications, like heroism and post hoc explanations about macrotrends. The pirate organizations of the seventeenth century significantly modified the trade norms in effect and the rules of governance on board ships. It was not one person's accomplishment. No heroic captain, no famous corsair

could claim to have played any significant role in the century-long historical trend described above. Pirate organizations are a sociopolitical phenomenon, not a group of isolated adventurers. And they are not all unified. In the seventeenth century, some pirate organizations challenged the Portuguese monopoly in order to replace it with its own; others never swayed from their cause against monopolies, and they all confronted other pirate organizations at one time or another. Where is the unity of the pirate class? Where is its so-called unique destiny? Nowhere. At the intermediate organizational level, however, it becomes possible to examine how pirates set their objectives and defend a public cause against accepted codes.

The legal analysis of the pirate phenomenon does not do justice to its power of economic transformation. Historical analysis misses the symmetry among pirate organizations through the ages. Also, the internal economic analysis of the pirate organization fails to provide a consistent explanation for the pirate phenomena across time and space. At best, it helps us understand why certain control and governance mechanisms were used over others. Its rationalist take on individual choices fails to capture the fundamentally uneconomic raison d'être of the pirate organization.

Toward an Orgology of Capitalism

Positioning our analysis at the level of the organization demonstrates how the normative variations introduced

by the pirate organization spread within the sovereign machine. These variations are combined within new sociotechnical arrangements, and pirates themselves become carriers of norms. The speed at which variations introduced by pirates spread within partially uncharted territory depends on several factors. When the pirate organization directly contributes to mapping out the territory—like the pirates of the seventeenth century who settled in the lands that they themselves discovered, or like Celera Genomics, which pioneered the deciphering of DNA—it can benefit from this good timing to take the initiative of normalization despite the protests of the sovereign. Also, when there is an easy path for the renegades to move freely between pirate and corsair organizations, one can also expect the changes to spread more quickly and easily, since they can directly infiltrate the code at the heart of the state. Lastly, when the mutations introduced tend to foster the survival and growth of the organizations adopting them, their presence becomes increasingly significant over time. For example, the democratic norm in effect on board pirate ships took on considerable evolutionary potential as it spread to mainland states.

We thus catch a glimpse of an evolutionary design of production systems. The states and organizations of the milieu continuously work to capture what has eluded them—namely, what pirate organizations take out or steal from gray areas. The sovereign redefines territory and overcodes norms of exchange and trade. The pirate organization decodes the evidence of capitalistic appropriation,

penetrates its core, and introduces variations into the code itself. Changes in the definition of trade norms are most often the outcome of the upheavals in the capitalist economy, following crises that destroy masses of overvalued assets. These recodings prompt the capitalistic organizations to turn against themselves. New laws then come to delineate the contours of the banking, the insurance, or the production systems. It is now time to consider competition as a contingent structure whose code depends on whether and how legitimate and renegade organizations confront one another.

So many thinkers denounce capitalism for its hyperindividualism, its pervasive reliance on marketing, the totalitarianism of its production modes that foster the enslavement of man, and its hijacking of "good" initiatives by "the system." These analyses oversimplify capitalism. They wrongly assume that a secret, hidden cause or coalition is running "the system." They rely on the convenient cliché of a Manichaean opposition between the market and the individual, the individual and the state, and the state and the market. They conceive of the collective as being masses, classes, strong and lasting, or tribes and networks that are flexible and fragile. We must go back from these abusive simplifications and investigate capitalism at the level of organizations. Today, we must try to understand the relationships between the social and business realities, organizations, and their constituent members.

Thus, we are calling for the development of an *"orgology"* of capitalism. Orgology, as a science about organizations,

would gather recent and multidisciplinary approaches from other social sciences, and investigate economic and societal issues, starting from the twofold observation that the world is increasingly complex in its organization, but also increasingly organizational in its structure—that is, dominated by organizations rather than individuals. Today, large multinational corporations, NGOs, private foundations, or industry associations have more power to influence the course of history than the European kings of the Middle Ages. But such organizations also face many more counterweights. An orgology of capitalism is thus required to understand how the world has changed and where it is heading. Borrowing from the methodologies of psychology, sociology, and economics, orgology as an organization science focuses on the emergence of organizations, their identity, their position in society, their growth strategies, and their evaluation by other societal actors. Instead of drawing an arbitrary line between the greedy businesspeople and the altruistic rebels, an orgology of capitalism seeks to explain how rebellious organizations can succeed in changing industry norms by having strategic leaders allocate resources cleverly. Instead of seeing corsairs as former pirates who are "selling out" (to the elites who run "the system"), an orgology of capitalism explains how and why corsair organizations actually help pirate organizations diffuse their social innovations at the heart of capitalism by creating a passage between the milieu and the fringes.

Leaving Utopia: Espousing the Continued Presence of Temporary Autonomous Organizations

Faced with the state that manufactures the reproduction of normative patterns within the sovereign territory, the pirate organization produces variations in every direction and tries to get out ahead of the sovereign. Ships with fewer weapons are faster, and surprise attacks catch the enemy unawares. A ship controlled directly by its crew does not need to wait for investors to collect enough capital to launch an expedition—and anything goes when it comes to gaining control of a ship without being accountable to the owners on land. By the same token, an organization that recopies a code already produced elsewhere, in order to outpace its rivals and design better software or a more complete map of the human genome, overtakes its direct competitors at a cost advantage.

The continuous and conflicting relationship between the state and the pirate organization means that capitalism never reproduces itself the same way twice. Moreover, capital does not grow in a homogeneous manner. It follows slopes and trajectories. It is guided from within territories by the relative power of the firms and organizations that foster its productiveness. Capitalist expansion is not unavoidable or directionless. Opening up the seas and space means entering into the unknown, yet it offers glimpses of the immense potential that lies out there. These horizons that the organizations step into are cleared

by a series of technoscientific upheavals: printing, maritime transport, electricity, airwaves, molecular biology, space, or cyberspace, all of which foster the will to rewrite the capitalistic norm. The torchbearers of these idealized visions of sharing the new are the pirate organizations. We are not holding the merits of pirate ideas above those of more legitimate businesses. What we want to show is the very nature of the workings of the capitalism-coding machines, endlessly deterritorializing and normalizing economic exchanges and profit, searching out the unknown for new territories to code, recognize, subjugate, and value.

The pirate organization is the necessary counterpart to capitalism. The production system based on private property and the protection of the property rights can only pursue its expansion by nurturing the pirate organization from the fringes of capitalism. What determines the pace of capitalistic evolution and rival production systems is competition between organizations of the milieu and pirate organizations. The former normalize trade based on legitimate appropriation rights. The latter enact alternative principles of value creation and capture. They express different property norms, including what we could call *legitimate expropriation on behalf of a public cause*.

The pirate organization marks the accursed part of capitalism that always eludes it. Driven into conquering unexplored horizons, irrepressibly marking and coding, defining and fencing in, capitalism is subjected to the opposing view of its inclusiveness—namely, to generate otherness, an organizational Other. The pirate organization

promotes an alternative public cause, which will eventually be surpassed. While utopias seek to create well-organized, peaceful, and long-standing spaces, the pirate organization promises little. Or rather it proposes a utopia-free world, constantly changing, never isolated, never centric, forever contingent, confrontational, and temporary.

NOTES

Chapter One

1. Toshiya Ueno, "Piracy Now and Then," http://nettime.org/
Lists-Archives/nettime-l-9810/msg00105.html. Ueno here refers to
Daniel Defoe, author of *Robinson Crusoe* (1719) and *A General History
of the Robberies and Murders of the Most Notorious Pirates* (1724); the
latter book was written by Captain Charles Johnson, an alleged pen
name of Defoe.

2. For information about the historical reconstruction of sea piracy
as a contemporary myth, see Martin Parker, "Pirates, Merchants and
Anarchists: Representations of International Business," *Management
and Organizational History* 4 (2009): 167–185.

Chapter Two

1. Readers interested in piracy should consult the bibliography at
the end of the book, which lists the main texts from which we have
developed our essay. The references considered to be less essential
for building an argument do not appear in the bibliography, which is
therefore nonexhaustive.

Chapter Three

1. Peter Sloterdijk, *La Palais de Cristal: A l'Intérieur du Capitalisme
Planétaire* (Paris: Maren Sell, 2006).

2. As Charles De Visscher emphasized, "The essential place of territory in the state organization and its highly symbolic meaning explain the proclivity … if not to identify the territory with the State, at least to contemplate its spatial definition as being inseparable from the sovereignty." Charles De Visscher, *Theory and Reality in Public International Law* (Paris: Pedone, 1953), 250.

3. The two volumes of *Capitalism and Schizophrenia* by Gilles Deleuze and Félix Guattari published in 1972 and 1980 (*L'Anti-Œdipe [Capitalisme et Schizophrénie]*, Paris: Les Éditions de Minuit, 1972, and *Mille Plateaux [Capitalisme et Schizophrénie 2]*, Paris: Les Éditions de Minuit, 1980) put forth an iconoclastic analysis of the modern state's formation and capitalist expansion. Their work paved the way for a theory of land-based globalization by extending beyond the limited framework of economic analysis. As Sloterdijk rightly pointed out, few philosophers dare to address the delicate task of tackling capitalism, which, nevertheless, happens to be the most consequential social phenomenon of our times. The importance of these texts is based on an essential observation that serves as a departure point for their authors: capitalism is neither a theory nor a treatise on liberty and its political consequences. Capitalism has not always existed, and there is no indication that it will never end.

4. Liberalism, in the classical sense used throughout the text, does not overlap with the current meaning of *liberal* in the United States. For an American reader, it would rather be a synonym for *libertarianism* or *neoliberalism*. To avoid confusion, we speak of the *liberalists* to refer to advocates of classical liberalism, who value individual freedom above everything else (and, importantly, not only *economic* freedom, as do recent proponents of neoliberalism).

5. See, for example, Jean-Claude Michéa, *The Realm of Lesser Evil: An Essay on Liberal Civilization* (Paris: Climats, 2008), and his critical examination of the minimal principles required for liberalism.

Chapter Four

1. Throughout the book, we use the term *corsair* to refer to organized groups committing acts of piracy in the name of a sovereign entity. Often, corsairs operating on the sea in the modern age are referred to as *privateers*. For the sake of consistency, we have decided to use the same term, *corsair*, for all types of territories—seas, airwaves, cyberspace, and DNA.

2. This paragraph was inspired by a chapter by Anne Pérotin-Dumon, "The Pirate and the Emperor," in J.D. Tracy (ed.), *The Political Economy of Merchant Empires: State Power and World Trade, 1350–1750* (Cambridge, UK; New York; Melbourne: Cambridge University Press, 1991), 196–227.

3. As Pérotin-Dumon says, "Since Antiquity, there has been a consensus that the pirate should be considered as a *hostis humani generis* and his offense an attack on the law of nations. But this general opinion has not been concretized as a tool of law; a proper 'law of nations' never existed." According to her, the definitional indeterminacy surrounding piracy still exists nowadays: "It appears that the conclusion of experts who discussed this at the time of the League of Nations (1919–1946) remains valid: There is no authoritative definition of international piracy." Ibid., 203.

4. This painting can be seen at the Philadelphia Museum of Art. The curious reader who lives too far away from Philly can take a look at it here: http://philamuseum.org/collections/permanent/102076.html.

5. In Pérotin-Dumon, "The Pirate and the Emperor," in J.D. Tracy (ed.), *The Political Economy of Merchant Empires* (Cambridge, UK; New York; Melbourne: Cambridge University Press, 1991), 204.

6. In Violet Barbour, "Privateers and Pirates of the West Indies," *American Historical Review*, 16:3 (1911): 529–566.

7. David E. Sanger, "Obama Order Sped Up Wave of Cyberattacks Against Iran," *New York Times*, June 1, 2012. This animation video about the inner workings of the Stuxnet virus is a must-see: http://vimeo.com/25118844.

8. David F. Marley, "The Lure of Spanish Gold," in David Cordingly (ed.), *Pirates* (North Dighton, UK: World Publications Group, 2005), 16–35.

9. David Cordingly, "Buccaneer Explorers," in Cordingly, *Pirates*, 62.

Chapter Five

1. Quoted, among others, by Hannah Arendt in *The Origins of Totalitarianism* (New York: Schocken Books, 1951). Rhodesia remained for long an unrecognized state after Cecil Rhodes's company acquired roughly 400,000 km² of land in the south of Africa in the late nineteenth century.

2. Jean Servier, *Histoire de l'Utopie* (Paris: Gallimard, Folio Essais, 1991).

3. A notable exception—and one that could start a war—concerns several large portions of unclaimed land located by the North Pole. Because global warming is making the corresponding underground resources increasingly accessible, several sovereign countries, including Canada, Russia, and Denmark, are now fighting over territorial control of these huge energy reserves.

4. Johan Schluter, Danish Anti-Piracy Group, quoted by Ryan Moffitt, "The Worst Part of Censorship Is [This Phrase Has Been Seized by Ice]," in *No Safe Harbor: Essay About Pirate Politics*, United States Pirate Party, CreateSpace.

5. This definition is that of Rodolphe Durand, *Organizational Evolution and Strategic Management* (London: Sage Publishers, 2006), 13. It refers to works in the field of "organization theory," as put into perspective, for instance, by Richard W. Scott, *Organizations: Rational, Natural, and Open Systems*, 5th ed. (Upper Saddle River, NJ: Prentice Hall, 2003).

Chapter Six

1. Marcus Rediker, *Between the Devil and the Deep Blue Sea: Merchant Seamen, Pirates and the Anglo-American Maritime World, 1700–1750* (Cambridge, UK: Cambridge University Press, 2004), 306.

2. *Calendar of State Papers, Colonial Series: America and West Indies*, vol. 1719–1720, no. 578 (London: National Archives, 1994), cited by David Cordingly (ed.), *Pirates* (North Dighton, UK: World Publications Group, 2005), 8.

3. An excerpt from Philip Gosse, *The History of Piracy* (Mineola, NY: Dover Publications, 1932); Marcus Rediker, *Between the Devil and the Deep Blue Sea*; and Peter Leeson, *The Invisible Hook: The Hidden Economics of Pirates* (Princeton, NJ: Princeton University Press, 2009).

4. Jean-Pierre Moreau, *Une Histoire des Pirates* (Paris: Tallandier, 2006), 69. Translated by the authors.

5. Ibid., 50–51.

6. Henning Hillman and Christina Gathmann, "Overseas Trade and the Decline of Privateering" (working paper, Department of Sociology, Stanford University, Stanford, CA, 2009).

7. Marcus Rediker, *Villains of All Nations: Atlantic Pirates in the Golden Age* (Boston: Beacon Press, 2004), 47.

8. Dian Murray, "Chinese Pirates," in Cordingly, *Pirates*, 212–235. See Gosse, *The History of Pirates*, 270–280, where the name of the pirate is Mrs. Ching.

9. Olivier Tesquet, *WikiLeaks: A True Account* (Paris: OWNIBOOKS Basics, 2011), 13. The quote is by Julian Assange, leader and founder of WikiLeaks.

Chapter Seven

1. See for instance the works of Peter T. Leeson on pirate organization and in particular his book entitled *The Invisible Hook: The Hidden Economics of Pirates* (Princeton, NJ: Princeton University Press, 2009).

2. The previous description reflects the organization of the most radical pirates of the time. Not all pirate crews were this extreme in their egalitarian practices.

3. This code was promulgated in 1721 and the first publication of it took place in 1724, in Charles Johnson, *A General History of the Robberies and Murders of the Most Notorious Pyrates*, London, 1724.

4. Leeson, *The Invisible Hook*, 43.

Chapter Eight

1. This chapter draws heavily on the book by Adrian Johns titled *Death of a Pirate: British Radio and the Making of the Information Age* (New York: W. W. Norton & Company, 2011).

2. Ibid., 18.

Chapter Nine

1. Femme S. Gaastra, *The Dutch East India Company: Expansion and Decline* (Leiden, the Netherlands: Walburg Pers, 2003), and Vitorino Magelhães Godinho, "The Portuguese and the 'Carreira da India,' 1497–1810," in J. R. Bruijn and F. S. Gaastra, (eds.), *Ships, Sailors and Spices* (Amsterdam: NEHA, 1993), 1–48.

2. Maurice Aymard (ed.), *Dutch Capitalism and World Capitalism* (Cambridge, UK: Cambridge University Press, 1982).

3. See, for instance, James D. Tracy, *The Political Economy of Merchant Empires: State Power and World Trade, 1350–1750* (Cambridge, UK: Cambridge University Press, 1991), 13.

4. Christopher Hill, *Liberty Against the Law: Some Seventeenth-Century Controversies* (London: Penguin Books, 1996), 115.

5. Adrian Johns, *Death of a Pirate: British Radio and the Making of the Information Age* (New York: W. W. Norton & Co., 2009).

6. Tim Jordan, *Hacking: Digital Media and Technological Determinism* (Cambridge, MA: Polity Press, 2008), 3.

7. Virginia Mayo, "Court Rules that Google-NSA Spy Ties Can Remain Secret," *USA Today*, May 12, 2012.

8. Andy Greenberg, "An Interview with Julian Assange," *Forbes*, November 29, 2010, http://www.forbes.com/sites/andygreenberg/2010/11/29/an-interview-with-wikileaks-julian-assange/.

9. For more information on the history of copyright in the publishing industry, we recommend the thorough and excellent book by Adrian Johns, *Piracy: The Intellectual Property Wars from Gutenberg to Gates* (Chicago: University of Chicago Press, 2010), and Rick Falkvinge's short and impactful "History of Copyright," in United States Pirate Party (eds), *No Safe Harbor: Essays About Pirate Politics*, CreateSpace, 146.

10. Rick Falkvinge, "History of Copryright," in *No Safe Harbor*. For an extensive history of copyright in the publishing industry, see the reference work by Adrian Johns, *Piracy*, cited just above.

Chapter Ten

1. The quote is from Adrian Johns, *Piracy: The Intellectual Property Wars from Gutenberg to Gates* (Chicago: University of Chicago Press, 2010), 491.

2. The verb *to hack* originally meant discovering an original and elegant solution to a complex technical problem, and whose distribution within a community wins it admiration by peers.

3. "Peer Production Communities Survey 2011," http://extreme.ajatukseni.net/2011/07/10/peer-production-communities-survey-2011, cited by owni.fr.

4. Apologies to our readers, but as is probably clear based on the particular context of the anti-indecency measures, deleting the F word in the text or replacing it with the politically correct "f——" would have been utterly self-defeating. The complete quote is available here: http://olografix.org/loris/open/manifesto.htm.

5. Bruce Sterling, *The Hacker Crackdown* (New York: Bantam Books, 1992), and Johan Söderberg, *Hacking Capitalism: The FOSS Software Movement* (New York: Routledge, 2008). See also the seminal work by Steven Levy, *Hackers: Heroes of the Computer Revolution* (Garden City, NJ: Doubleday, 1984).

6. Excerpts from a hacker manifesto written by Digital Ebola and available at http://web.textfiles.com/ezines/KV/kv12.txt.

7. Scott J. Henderson, *The Dark Visitor: Inside the World of Chinese Hackers*, 2007, available at http://www.scribd.com/doc/24587105/The-Dark-Visitor-Scott-J-Henderson.

8. The first quote comes from Wikipedia, http://en.wikipedia.org/wiki/Chaos_Computer_Club. The second quote is a summary of the CCC's objectives according to Daniel Domscheit-Berg, CCC member, former spokesperson for WikiLeaks, and founder of Open-Leaks. It can be found in Olivier Tesquet, *WikiLeaks: A True Account* (OWNIBOOKS Basics, 2011); the e-book can be purchased or "hacked" here: http://shop.owni.fr/fr/43-wikileaks-a-true-account.html.

Chapter Eleven

1. Johan Söderberg, *Hacking Capitalism: The FOSS Software Movement* (New York: Routledge, 2008), 3.

2. Adrian Johns, *Piracy: The Intellectual Property Wars from Gutenberg to Gates* (Chicago: University of Chicago Press, 2010). The NEC story is mentioned in chapter 1. For a thorough discussion on the difference between patents and copyrights, see chapter 10.

3. People refer to them as *patent sharks* as well: Joachim Henkel and Markus Reitzig, "Patent Sharks," *Harvard Business Review*, June 2008, 129–133.

4. Timo Fischer and Joachim Henkel, "Patent Trolls on Markets for Technology: An Empirical Analysis of Trolls' Patent Acquisitions," working paper, TUM, Munich, 2009.

Chapter Twelve

1. Michael T. Hannan and John Freeman, *Organizational Ecology* (Cambridge, MA: Harvard University Press, 1989).

2. Marie-Laure Djelic and Rodolphe Durand, "Strong in the Morning, Dead in the Evening: A Genealogical and Contextual

Perspective on Organizational Selection," in J. Baum and J. Lampel (eds.), *The Globalization of Strategy Research: Advances in Strategic Management* (East Sussex, UK: Emerald, 2010).

3. See the work of Frank Dobbin and Timothy Dowds (e.g., "How Policy Shapes Competition: Early Railroad Foundings in Massachusetts," *Administrative Science Quarterly* 42 (1997): 501–529, and "The Market that Antitrust Built: Public Policy, Private Coercion, and Railroad Acquisitions, 1825–1922," *American Sociological Review* 65 (2000): 631–657.

4. This quote is taken from Dobbin and Dowd, "The Market that Antitrust Built," 634.

5. Bruce Sterling, *The Hacker Crackdown* (New York: Bantam Books, 1992).

Chapter Thirteen

1. Frédéric Dardel and Renaud Leblond, *Main Basse sur le Génome* (Paris: Anne Carrière, 2008).

2. Digital Ebola, *Keen Veracity* (e-zine), www.legions.org.

3. Heather Lowrie and Joyce Tait, *Guidelines for the Appropriate Risk Governance of Synthetic Biology*, International Risk Governance Council policy brief (Edinburgh, Geneva: IRGC, 2010), irgc.org; and Stew Magnuson, "Growing Public Interest in Genetic Science Sparks Some Bio-Security Concerns," *National Defense Magazine*, June 2010.

4. Markus Schmidt, "Diffusion of Synthetic Biology: A Challenge to Biosafety," *Systems and Synthetic Biology* 2 (2008): 1–6.

5. Andrew Pollack, "U.S. Says Genes Should Not Be Eligible for Patents," *New York Times*, October 29, 2010, http://nytimes.com/2010/10/30/business/30drug.html?_r=1&ref=science. Although the brief was released on the day this book was first published in French, the authors had nothing to do with it.

6. Andrew Mushita and Carol B. Thompson, *Biopiracy of Biodiversity: Global Exchange as Enclosure* (Trenton, NJ: Africa World Press, 2007).

7. Daniel Heller-Roazen, *L'Ennemi de Tous: Le Pirate Contre les Nations* (Paris, Seuil, 2010).

Chapter Fourteen

1. Prince Roy, "About Sealand," http://www.sealandgov.org.

BIBLIOGRAPHY

Aymard, Maurice. "Introduction," in *Dutch Capitalism and World Capitalism*, ed. Maurice Aymard. Cambridge, UK: Cambridge University Press, 1982, 1–10; Paris: Éditions de la Maison des Sciences de l'Homme.

Barbour, Violet. "Privateers and Pirates of the West Indies." *American Historical Review* 16, no. 3 (1911): 529–566.

————. "Dutch and English Merchant Shipping in the Seventeenth Century." *Economic History Review* 2, no. 2 (1930): 261–290.

Bey, Hakim. *TAZ: Zone Autonome Temporaire*. Paris: Editions de l'Eclat, 1997. Originally published as *T.A.Z.: The Temporary Autonomous Zone, Ontological Anarchy, Poetic Terrorism* (Autonomedia, 1991).

Borschberg, Peter. "Hugo Grotius' Theory of Trans-Oceanic Trade Regulation: Revisiting *Mare Liberum*." *International Law and Justice* working paper 2005/14, 2005. http://www.iilj.org.

Brady Jr., Thomas A. "The Rise of Merchant Empires, 1400–1700." In Tracy, *The Political Economy of Merchant Empires*, 1991, 117–160.

Chaudhuri, K. N. "Reflections on the Organizing Principle of Pre-Modern Trade." In Tracy, *The Political Economy of Merchant Empires*, 1991, 421–442.

Cordingly, David, ed. *Pirates: Terror on the High Seas—From the Caribbean to the South China Sea*. North Dighton, UK: World Publications Group, 2005.

————. "Buccaneer Explorers." In Cordingly, *Pirates*, 58–75.

————. "Introduction." In Cordingly, *Pirates*, 6–15.

Dardel, F., and R. Leblond. *Main Basse sur le Génome*. Paris: Anne Carrière, 2008.

Defoe, Daniel. *A General History of the Pyrates*, [1724]. Mineola, NY: Courier Dover Publications, 1999.

Deleuze, Gilles, and Félix Guattari. *L'Anti-Œdipe (Capitalisme et Schizophrénie)*. Paris: Les Éditions de Minuit, 1972.

———. *Anti-Oedipus*. Vol. 1, *Capitalism & Schizophrenia*. London: Continuum, 2004.

———. *A Thousand Plateaus*. Vol. 2, *Capitalism & Schizophrenia*. London: Continuum. 2004. Originally published as *Mille Plateaux, Capitalisme et Schizophrénie 2* (Paris: Les Éditions de Minuit, 1980).

De Visscher, Charles. *Théories et Réalités en Droit International Public*. Paris: Pedone, 1953.

———. *Theory and Reality in Public International Law* (Princeton, NJ: Princeton University Press, 1957).

Djelic, Marie-Laure, and Rodolphe Durand. "Strong in the Morning, Dead in the Evening: A Genealogical and Contextual Perspective on Organizational Selection." In *The Globalization of Strategy Research: Advances in Strategic Management*, edited by J. Baum and J. Lampel. East Sussex, UK: Emerald, 2010.

Dobbin, Frank, and Timothy Dowds. "How Policy Shapes Competition: Early Railroad Foundings in Massachusetts." *Administrative Science Quarterly* 42 (1997): 501–529.

———. "The Market that Antitrust Built: Public Policy, Private Coercion, and Railroad Acquisitions, 1825–1922." *American Sociological Review* 65 (2000): 631–657.

Durand, Rodolphe. *Entreprise et Évolution Économique*. Editions Belin, 2000.

———. *Organizational Evolution and Strategic Management*. London: Sage Publishers, 2006.

Esquemelin, Alexander O. *The Buccaneers of America*. [1678]. Mineola, NY: Courier Dover Publications, 2000. http://www.loc.gov/flash/pagebypage/buccaneers/bookBorder.html.

Fischer, Timo, and Joachim Henkel. "Patent Trolls on Market for Technology, an Empirical Analysis of Trolls' Patent Acquisitions." Working paper, Technische Universität München, 2009.

Gaastra, Femme S. *The Dutch East India Company: Expansion and Decline*. Leiden, The Netherlands: Walburg Pers, 2003.

Gosse, Philip. *The History of Piracy*. [1932]. Mineola, NY: Dover Publications, 2007.

Hannan, Michael T., and John Freeman. *Organizational Ecology*. Cambridge, MA: Harvard University Press, 1989.

Heller-Roazen, Daniel. *L'Ennemi de Tous: Le Pirate Contre les Nations*. Paris: Seuil, 2010. Originally published as *The Enemy of All: Piracy and the Law of Nations* (Cambridge, MA: Zone Books, 2009).

Henderson, Scott J. *The Dark Visitor: Inside the World of Chinese Hackers*. First Publishers, 2007.

Hillmann, Henning, and Christina Gathmann. "Overseas Trade and the Decline of Privateering." Working paper, Stanford University, 2009.

Hill, Christopher. "Radical Pirates?" In *The Origins of Anglo-American Radicalism*, edited by Maragret C. Jacob and James R. Jacob. London: Allen & Unwin, 1984, 17–32.

———. *Liberty Against the Law: Some Seventeenth-Century Controversies*. London: Penguin Books, 1996.

Holton, Robert J. *The Transition from Feudalism to Capitalism*. London: MacMillan, 1985.

International Risk Governance Council. Concept notes, *Synthetic Biology*, 2008, irgc.org.

The Invisible Committee. *The Coming Insurrection*. Los Angeles: Semiotext(e), 2009. Originally published as Comité Invisible, *L'insurrection qui Vient* (Paris: La Fabrique Editions, 2007).

Israel, Jonathan I. *Dutch Primacy in World Trade, 1585–1740*. New York: Oxford University Press, 1989.

Johns, Adrian. *Piracy: The Intellectual Property Wars from Gutenberg to Gates*. Chicago: University of Chicago Press, 2010.

———. *Death of a Pirate: British Radio and the Making of the Information Age*. New York: W. W. Norton & Co., 2009.

Jordan, Tim. *Hacking: Digital Media and Technological Determinism*. Cambridge, MA: Polity Press, 2008.

Leeson, Peter T. *The Invisible Hook: The Hidden Economics of Pirates*. Princeton, NJ: Princeton University Press, 2009.

———. "An-*arrgh*-chy: The Law and Economics of Pirate Organization." *Journal of Political Economy* 115, no. 6 (2007): 1049–1094.

Lemisch, Jesse. "Jack Tar in the Streets: Merchant Seamen in the Politics of Revolutionary America." *William and Mary Quarterly* 25 (1968): 371–407.

Levy, Steven. *Hackers: Heroes of the Computer Revolution*. New York: Penguin, 1984.

Lucie-Smith, Edward. *Outcasts of the Sea*. New York: Paddington Press, 1978.

Lydon, James. *Pirates, Privateers, and Profit*. Upper Saddle River, NJ: Gregg Press, 1970.

Magelhães Godinho, V. "The Portuguese and the 'Carreira da India,' 1497–1810." In *Ships, Sailors and Spices*, edited by J.R. Bruijn and F. S. Gaastra. Amsterdam: NEHA, 1993, 1–48.

Marley, David F. "The Lure of Spanish Gold," In Cordingly, *Pirates*, 16–35.

Marx, Jenifer G. "Brethen of the Coast." In Cordingly, *Pirates*, 36–57.

Mason, Matt. *A Pirate's Dilemma*. New York: Free Press, 2008.

Michéa, Jean-Claude. *Essai sur le Moindre Mal*. Climats, 2008.

Moreau, Jean-Pierre. *Une Histoire des Pirates*. Paris: Tallandier, 2006.

Murray, Dian H. "Chinese Pirates." In Cordingly, *Pirates*, 212–235.

Mushita, A., and Carol B. Thompson. *Biopiracy of Biodiversity: Global Exchange as Enclosure*. Trenton, NJ: Africa World Press, 2007.

National Defense Magazine. "Growing Public Interest in Genetic Science Sparks Some Bio-Security Concerns." June 2010, http://nationaldefensemagazine.org.

Ormrod, David. *The Rise of Commercial Empires: England and the Netherlands in the Age of Mercantilism, 1650–1770*. Cambridge, UK: Cambridge University Press, 2003.

Pérotin-Dumon, Anne. "The Pirate and the Emperor." In Tracy, *The Political Economy of Merchant Empires*, 1991, 196–227.

Rediker, Marcus. *Between the Devil and the Deep Blue Sea: Merchant Seamen, Pirates and the Anglo-American Maritime World, 1700–1750*. [1987]. Cambridge, UK: Cambridge University Press, 2004.

———. "Libertalia: The Pirates's Utopia." In Cordingly, *Pirates*, 124–139.

Ritchie, Robert C. *Captain Kidd and the War Against the Pirates*. Cambridge, MA: Harvard University Press, 1986.

Schmidt, Markus. "Diffusion of Synthetic Biology: A Challenge to Biosafety." *Systems and Synthetic Biology* 2 (2008): 1–6.

Scott, W. Richard. *Organizations: Rational, Natural, and Open Systems*, 5th ed. Upper Saddle River; NJ: Prentice Hall, 2003.

Servier, Jean. *Histoire de l'Utopie*. Paris: Gallimard, Folio Essais, 1991.

Sloterdijk, Peter. *La Palais de Cristal: A l'Intérieur du Capitalisme Planétaire*. Paris: Maren Sell, 2006.

Söderberg, Johan. *Hacking Capitalism: The FOSS Software Movement*. New York: Routledge, 2008.

Sterling, Bruce. *The Hacker Crackdown*. New York: Bantam Books, 1992.

Tesquet, Olivier. *WikiLeaks: A True Account*. Paris: OWNIBOOKS Basics, 2011.

Tracy, James D., ed. *The Political Economy of Merchant Empires: State Power and World Trade, 1350–1750*. Cambridge, UK; New York; Melbourne: Cambridge University Press, 1991.

———. "Introduction." In Tracy, *Political Economy of Merchant Empires*, 1991.

Van Creveld, Martin. *The Rise and Fall of the State*. Oxford: Oxford University Press, 2002.

Vergne, J. P. "Machinerie Mercantiliste: Capitalisme et Piraterie." Master's thesis, University Paris-I, Panthéon-Sorbonne, 2006.

———. "Case of the Dutch East India Company, 1602–1800." Best Papers Proceedings, Academy of Management, Anaheim, CA, 2008.

Wark, McKenzie. *A Hacker Manifesto*. Cambridge, MA: Harvard University Press, 2004.

Weber, Max. *L'Éthique Protestante et l'Esprit du Capitalisme*. [1905]. Paris: Pocket/Agora, 1989.

Zizek, Slavoj. *Organes sans Corps: Deleuze et consequences*. Paris: Èditions Amsterdam, 2008.

INDEX

absolutism, 27. *See also* sovereignty
   and sovereign states
Acacia, 117–118
accounting methods, 75–76, 89
administrative norms, 89
Agreement on Trade-Related
   Aspects of Intellectual
   Property Rights, 138
agriculture, enclosure and,
   22–23
Alexander the Great, 11–12
Alsthom, 123, 127–128
Altman, Mitch, 104–105
Amazon, 143
Amnesty International, 47
Amsterdam Stock Market, 25,
   31, 89
Anonymous, 14, 47, 97, 108, 143
Anti-Counterfeiting Trade
   Agreement (ACTA)
   (2012), 151
Anti-Oedipus (Deleuze and
   Guattari), 41
Arpanet, 50–51, 94–95
Assange, Julian, 52, 97

assimilation, 66
asulia, 29
asylum zones, 29
AT&T, 91, 95, 96, 130–132
Augustine, Saint, 11–12
authority, 54, 73

banks and banking, 23, 124, 146
Barbour, Violet, 35
Barlow, John Perry, 27–28, 101,
   107, 109
BASIC, 105–106
BBC. *See* British Broadcasting
   Corporation (BBC)
Bellamy, Samuel, 61–62
Bellomont, Earl of, 35
Bennett, Colonel, 64
biopiracy, 7, 14, 48–49,
   133–143. *See also* genetic
   engineering
biopolitics, 140
biosecurity, 136–137
Blackbeard, 62
BlackBerry, 117

Blair, Tony, 134
blue boxes, 131
Blu-ray Disc Association, 53
brain drain, 22
British Broadcasting Corporation (BBC), 6, 67, 81–85, 91
Radio One, 92–93
British South Africa Company, 41, 149
buccaneers, 12–13
bureaucracy, 54

Canudos, 43–44, 51
capital
deterritorialization of, 18–19, 20–23
in economic exchanges, 24
capitalism
in China, 27
competition and, 124–132
countermodel of pirates to, 65–66
Darwinian, 124–127
defining, 2–3
deterritorialization and, 20–23
emergence of, 18–19
evolution of, 25–26, 57, 69, 150–152, 156
expansion of, 14–15, 161–162
focus on markets and individuals and, 4, 17–19, 159
future of the state and, 145–152
genetic engineering and, 139–143
gray areas in, 85

intellectual property rights and, 114–116
liberalism versus, 27–28, 96–99
monopolies and, 6, 89–90
neoclassical economic theory and, 18
normalization and, 43
opposition to, 123–124
orgology of, 8, 157–160
piracy forms and, 5
pirate organizations and, 155–156
pivotal periods in, 1
public cause and, 65–69
scope and nature of, 2–3
self-destruction of, 2, 152
sovereignty and, 3, 19–21, 28, 143
Caribbean, piracy in, 12–13
Carreira da India, 88–89
cartels, 128–131
Celera Genomics, 133, 134–137, 158
censorship, 46, 98, 107
Central Intelligence Agency (CIA), 14
chain of command, 72, 73–74
Chamberlain, Neville, 84
Chanel, Coco, 53
Chaos Computer Club, 110
charters, 44, 87–88, 88–89
Chen I Sao, 64
child pornography, 46
China
capitalism in, 27
Confederation of the Six Flags and, 64
cyberpirates in, 35–37

digital content filtering by, 46
Google attack from, 96
Kazakhstan lease with,
149–150
Moon exploration by, 141
patent registrations in, 116
Cicero, 10
Citigroup, 14
citizenship, 147–152
city-states, 9, 12,
19–20. *See also* nation-states;
sovereignty and sovereign
states
Civil War, 128–129
Clinton, Bill, 134
Clinton, Hillary, 96
Clonaid, 48–49, 135, 146
cloning, 48
Coase, Ronald, 91
"Code Is Law" (Lessig), 101
codes of conduct, 74–76
coinage, 23
Columbus, Christopher, 4–5
commoditization, 85
competition, 123–132
    Darwinian, 124–127
    forms of, organization
        selection and, 126–132
    monopolies and, 126–132
    pirate organizations and, 155
    pirates in, 63–64
Confederation of the Six Flags, 64
Conselheiro, Antonio, 43–44, 51
control, 42, 72
Convention of Biodiversity, 138
copyright law, 98–99,
    111–112. *See also* intellectual
    property rights

corsairs, 29–39
    biocorsair organizations,
        134–138
    cyperspace, 37
    Hague Peace Conference
        on, 67
    letters of marque and, 34–37
    norms diffusion by, 160
    pirate organizations and,
        55–57
    pirates distinguished from,
        32–34, 37–39, 57, 59–60
    warfare and, 60–61
Council of Trade and
    Plantations, 64
counterfeiting, 13, 114–115, 151
Craig Venter Institute (CVI),
    135–136
Crick, Francis, 48
criminal gangs, 56
criminalization, 56–57
culture dissemination, 92
currency, 23
custom of the coast, 74–76
CVI, 143
cyberpiracy, 6–7, 14, 123
    actions in, 94–95
    content filtering and, 46–47
    corsairs and, 37, 38
    digital rights management
        and, 112
    hacking versus, 104–105
    Honker Union of China,
        35–37
    manifestos in, 108–109
    monopolies and, 93–96
    origins of, 27–28, 104–106
    politicization of, 107–108

cyberspace, 101–110
defining status of, 42
filtering content in, 46
freeware and, 102–103
network connections in, 106
normalization of, 45–47,
93–96
origins of, 50–51
piracy in, 104–106
sovereignty in, 106–110
web stations, 93
cyberwarfare, 6, 37

da Gama, Vasco, 88
Dampier, William, 38
DataTreasury, 117–118
debt crises, 146–147
De Civitate Dei (Saint
Augustine), 11–12
Declaration of Paris (1856), 67
"Declaration of the Independence
of Cyberspace, A" (Barlow),
27–28, 101, 107, 109
decoding, 67
Defoe, Daniel, 59
Deleuze, Gilles, 41
democratic elections, 74, 76–79
deterritorialization, 18–19
capitalism and, 20–23
genetic engineering and,
142–143
monopolies and, 97–98
nation-states and, 145–152
patent trolls and, 117–121
of states, 148–152
Detoeuf, Auguste, 123, 127–128
Digital Ebola, 135

Digital Millennium Copyright
Act, 108
digital rights management
(DRM) systems, 112
digital territory. *See* cyberpiracy;
cyberspace
discovery, desire for, 55
"DIYbio" movement, 137
DNA, 42, 133–143. *See also*
genetic engineering
normalization of, 47–49
patenting, 137–139
Dolly (cloned sheep), 48
Dotcom, Kim, 94
Drake, Francis, 34, 38

East India Companies, 6, 26,
87–88, 89, 91
corsairs and, 30–32
monopoly of, 124–125, 126, 156
eBay, 115
ecological perspective on
capitalism, 124–127, 158–159
economic exchange
hierarchy of among pirates,
72–73
intellectual property rights
and, 114–116
legitimization of forms of, 22
monopolies and, 88
normalization of, 23–26
norms of, 7
patent trolls and, 117–121
piracy and, 71–79
pirate organizations and, 155
economic selection, 124–127
Edison, Thomas, 53

Electronic Frontier Foundation, 107, 108, 109
Elizabeth I, queen of England, 38
e-mail, 94–95
enclosure, 22–23, 102–103
Enemy of All, The (Heller-Roazen), 17
Enlightenment, 78
equality, 76–79
Eurogroup, 146–147
European Parliament, 151
European Patent Office (EPO), 114, 116, 118
exclusion, right of, 113–116
expansionism, 17–28. See also sovereignty and sovereign states
   boundary creation and, 41–42
   common good and, 66
   deterritorialization and, 23, 148–152
   genetic engineering and, 141–143
   gray areas and, 85
   intellectual property laws and, 94
   intellectual property rights and, 114–116
   monopolies and, 6, 87–99
   normalization and, 43–44
   piracy and, 4–5, 14–15
   pirate organizations and, 55–57
   pirates versus corsairs and, 30–39
   sovereignty and, 148–152
   warfare and, 50–51

Federal Bureau of Investigation (FBI), 94
feudalism, 19, 20
   deterritorialization and, 20–21
Feynman, Richard, 133, 136
financial crises of 2008 and 2011, 25, 146–147
fiscal standards, 42
Fischer, Timo, 118
Flame virus, 37
Fleury, Captain, 62–63
flibustiers, 60
Florida Pirate Party, 123
Florin, Captain, 32–33
Forgent, 117–118
Foucault, Michel, 140
franchises, 150
freedom of the seas, 66–67, 83, 125
Freedom of the Seas (Grotius), 66–67
free expression, 103, 105–106, 146
free market economics, 127–128
Free Software Foundation, 103, 107
free trade, 22, 27

gangs, criminal, 56
Gates, Bill, 52, 105–106
genetic engineering, 42, 133–143
   corsairs and pirates in, 134–137
   evolution of capitalism and, 139–143
   normalization of, 47–49
   public cause and, 137–139

geography
  aerial, 45
  concrete, 43–44
  space and, 47–50
  virtual, 45–47
globalization, 99, 154
  cyberspace and, 110
  monopolies and, 90
gold rush, 22
Google, 94, 96, 143
Gordon, Nathaniel, 13
Gosse, Philip, 9
Great Britain
  copyright law, 98
  enclosure in, 22–23
  impact of piracy on, 63, 64
  pirate radio and, 81–85
Grotius, Hugo, 66–67
Guattari, Félix, 41
guilds, 20
Gulf of Aden, 13
Gutenberg, Johannes, 53

Hacker Crackdown, The
  (Sterling), 131
hackers, 94–95, 104–105.
  See also cyberpiracy
  crackdown on, 107
  intellectual property rights
    and, 114–121
  phone phreaks, 131–132
Hacking Capitalism
  (Söderberg), 87
Hague Peace Conference
  (1907), 67
HavenCo, 148
hedge funds, 146

Heller-Roazen, Daniel, 17, 139
Henderson, Scott, 110
Henkel, Joachim, 118
heroism, 156–157
Hill, Christopher, 90
historiography
  on corsairs versus pirates, 35
  on economics of piracy, 71–72
  on piracy, 3
Hoffman, Abbie, 27
holding companies, 129
Homebrew Computer Club,
  104, 105–106
Honker Union of China, 35–37
Huguenots, 22
Human Genome Project,
  134–137, 141

ICANN, 45–46
Iceland Modern Media
  Initiative, 146
identity, 57
Indies, route to the, 88–90
individuals
  focus on in capitalism, 4,
    17–19, 159
  free market economics and, 27
  impact of organizations versus,
    52–53, 156, 157
industrial property, 113–116.
  See also intellectual
    property rights
InfraGard, 37
innovation, patent trolls and,
  117–121
insurance companies, 23,
  89–90, 146

intellectual property rights, 7
  copyright law and, 98–99
  cyberspace and, 93–94
  genetic engineering and,
    47–49, 137–139
  pirate radio and, 84
  right of exclusion and, 113–116
  trolls and, 116–121, 125
interdisciplinary approach, 5, 8
International Broadcasting
  Corporation (IBC), 82–83
international law, 32
  on freedom of the seas, 66–67
  monopolies and, 89
International Maritime
  Organization, 13
Internet, 45–46, 50–51, 93.
  See also cyberspace
interventionism, 127–128

Jefferson, Thomas, 134
Jenkins, Hugh, 81
Jobs, Steve, 105, 131
Johns, Adrian, 92
Jolly Roger, 77

Kant, Immanuel, 145, 150
Kazakhstan, 149–150
Kidd, Captain William, 35, 36
KSR v. Teleflex, 120

labor, deterritorialization of,
  18–19, 20–21, 20–23
law of reprisals, 11, 29, 65
Leeson, Peter, 71–72, 76–77

Legions of the Underground, 47,
  51, 108–109
legitimacy, 7–8
  of economic exchanges, 22
  normalization and, 42–43
  public cause and, 69, 162
Lessig, Lawrence, 101
letters of marque and reprisal,
  34–37, 60–61
liberalism, 27–28, 96–99
licenses, 102
Licensing Act (1662), 98–99
Lockheed Martin, 37
Lulz Security, 14, 47

macrotrends, 156–157
management, 54
Manning, Bradley, 37
markets
  focus on, 4, 159
  free market economics and, 27
Mary I, queen of England, 98
Masaccio, 33
MasterCard, 97
MedImmune v. Genentech, 120
Megaupload, 94
merchant marine, 78
mergers and acquisitions, 129–130
Microsoft, 52, 96, 111
milieu, organizations of the, 7,
  68, 141–143, 152
Moffitt, Ryan, 123
Moilanen, Jarkko, 104
monopolies, 87–99
  antitrust law and, 128–131
  chartered companies and, 44,
    87–88

cyberspace and, 93–96
liberalism and, 96–99
natural, 129–132
norms diffused by, 91–93
patent trolls and, 118–121
pirate competition with,
63–64
pirate radio and, 6
public cause and, 67
radio, 81–85
in radio, 81–85, 91–93
software, 111
the state in, 22
Monsanto, 97, 143
Morgan, Henry, 62
Morgan, J. P., 128–129
MP3 standard, 53–54
multinational organizations, 31,
145–152, 160
Musk, Elon, 50
mutiny, 73
mycoplasma laboratorium,
135–136

Napster, 53–54, 94
NASA, 36
National Institutes of Health,
134–137, 138–139
nationality, 57
National Security Agency
(NSA), 96
nation-states, 8, 142–152.
See also sovereignty and
sovereign states
Native Americans, relocation
of, 22
NEC Corporation, 114

neoclassical economic theory, 18
nongovernmental organizations
(NGOs), 107–108, 160
normalization, 18–19
capitalism and nature of, 28
chartered companies and, 44
competition and, 127–128, 132
creation of pirates and, 52–53
of cyberspace, 93–96
decoding, 67
of economic exchanges, 22,
23–26
of genetic engineering,
140–143
inclusion/exclusion and, 51
monopolies in, 87–92
of natural spaces, 43–44
organizations in, 157–160
pirate organizations and,
50–51, 53–57, 65, 79
public good and, 65–69
of risk, 23
seventeenth-century, 26
territorial, 50–51
of territories, 41–42
of trade and deterritorialization, 22–23
norms, 7, 50–51, 153
corsairs and, 29, 160
in cyberspace, 110
diffusion of, 53–54
genetic engineering, 140–143
monopolies and, 89–90
organizational, 54
overcoding of, 24–25
patent trolls and, 117–121
pirate versus sovereign state,
10–11, 15, 77–78

property rights and, 11
societal, 24–25
NTP, 117

Obama, Barack, 6, 37
Old Brazilian Republic, 43–44
oligopolies, 121, 129
open source software, 95
organization
context and, 126–131
of international trade, 19–20
of pirates, 2, 71–79
of pirates versus corsairs,
38–39
of society, 24–25
Organization for Economic
Cooperation and Develop-
ment (OECD), 14
organizations
competition and selection of,
126–132
definition of, 54
focus on markets and individuals versus, 4, 52–53
identity in, 57
influence of, 53–54
of the milieu, 7, 68, 141–143,
152
orgology of capitalism and, 8,
157–160
orgology of capitalism, 8, 157–160
Outer Space Treaty (1967),
49–50
outsider status, 55
overcoding, 24–25
in cyberspace, 46
pirate organizations and, 79

Page, Larry, 50
pamphleteering, 98
Panasonic, 53
patents, 113–116
biogenetics and, 137–139
growth in numbers of, 116
pooling, 115
Patriot Act, 108
Peace of Utrecht (1713), 61
penal standards, 42
Pérotin-Dumon, Anne, 87
perspective, 32–34, 59–60
pharmaceuticals, 115
Philips, 53
phone phreaks, 131–132
Phrack magazine, 106
"Pirate and the Emperor, The"
(Pérotin-Dumon), 87
pirate organizations, 2, 41–57
as countermodel, 65–66
criminal gangs distinguished
from, 56
in cyberspace, 6–7, 101–110
definition of, 52–57
economic exchanges and, 88
evolution of, 154
in evolution of capitalism,
57, 69
fair competition and,
123–132
future of, 151–152, 161–163
influence of, 151
lack of homogeneity in, 78
monopolies and, 87–99
nationality and, 57
norms challenged by, 54–55,
157–160
origins of, 59–69

overcoding and, 79
patent trolls, 117–121
public cause and, 65–69
public cause of, 5
self-definition of, 65
sovereignty and, 147–148
strategies of, 55
territorial expansion and,
    17–28
territorial normalization and,
    50–51
warfare and, 60–61
pirate radio, 6, 14, 67, 81–85
    corsairs, 38
    normalization and, 45, 92–93
pirates and piracy
    in ancient times, 10–12
    bio-, 7
    chain of command in, 72,
        73–74
    codes of, 74–76
    collective memory of, 2
    corsairs distinguished from,
        29–39, 59–60
    crew size of, 61–62
    in cyberspace, 6–7
    definition of, 2, 9–10
    economics of, 71–79
    extent of, 61–64
    forms of, 5
    golden ages of, 12–15, 44
    hierarchy of, 72–76
    high-seas, 12–14, 59–67
    impact of, 7
    interdisciplinary approach
        to, 5
    norms in, 10–11
    organization of, 61–64, 71–79

perspective on, 32–34
pivotal role of, 1
property rights and, 11–12
sovereignty and, 3, 154
threat of, 15
traits of, 2, 14–15
uncharted territory and, 56–57
warfare and, 60–61
Planetary Resources, 50
Plugge, Leonard, 83
Pompey, 11
PowerPoint, 103
privateering, 67
privateers. See corsairs
prize law, 11
production systems, evolution
    of, 158–159
property rights, 11–12. See also
    intellectual property rights
    licenses and, 102
    outer space and, 49–50
    piracy and, 77–78
    pirate organizations and, 88
    sovereignty and, 19–20
public cause, 5, 65–69, 162
    cyberspace and, 93–96, 103,
        110
    genetic engineering and,
        137–139, 141
    intellectual property rights
        and, 113–116
    maritime law and, 125
    monopolies and, 88
    software and, 112

quartermasters, 74, 75–76
Queen Anne's Revenge (ship), 62

radio, monopolies in, 81–85, 91–93
Radio Luxembourg, 83–84
Radio Mercur, 83, 84
Radio Nordzee, 45, 51
Radio One, 92–93
Raelian Cloning Clinic, 48–49
recruiting, 55, 89
Rediker, Marcus, 63
reductionism, 5
Rembrandt Technologies, 117–118
Research In Motion (RIM), 117
resources, deterritorialization of, 18–19, 20–23, 24
reterritorialization, 22
Rhodes, Cecil, 41, 149
risk, normalization of, 23, 89–90
Roberts, Bartholomew, 38, 62, 74–75
Rockefeller, John D., 128–129
Roy, Prince, 147–148
Royal African Company, 64

Saint Francis Receiving the Stigmata (Van Eyck), 33
Samsung, 53
San Francisco Rail Agency, 108
Santa Catarina (ship), 30–32
Schmidt, Markus, 137
Science (journal), 136
Sealand, 147–148
Secret Service, 107
separation of powers, 74, 76–79
Sherman Antitrust Act (1890), 128–131
Shuttleworth, Mark, 111

Siegen military academy, 89
signaling theory, 77
Simonyi, Charles, 50
slaves, 77
slave trade, 63–64, 78
Sloterdijk, Peter, 153
social contract, 115
social insurance, 76–79
social interaction norms, 7, 24–25, 42
individuals and, 156, 157
organizations and, 54
Söderberg, Johan, 87
software. See also cyberpiracy
freeware, 102–103
intellectual property rights and, 111–112
licensing, 102
open source, 95
Somali pirates, 13–14
Sony, 14, 53
sovereignty and sovereign states, 3
capitalism and, 19–21, 143
citizenship and, 147–152
competition and, 127–128
corsairs and, 29–39
cybercorsairs and, 36–37
cyberspace and, 106–110
definition of, 23–24
deterritorialization and, 20–21
deterritorialization of, 148–152
franchises and, 150
future of, 145–152
genetic engineering and, 138–139, 141–143
legitimacy and, 7–8
metasovereignty and, 160

monopolies and, 95–99
normalization of exchanges
  by, 23–26, 42–43
norms imposed by, 24–25
outer space and, 49–50
overcoding by, 24–25
pirate organizations and, 56
pirate radio and, 83–85
pirate relationship with, 14–15
pirates distinguished from,
  11–12
pirates versus corsairs and,
  29–39
power differentials among, 39
property rights and, 19–20
public cause and, 69
Sealand, 147–148
warfare and, 60–61
space, outer, 42, 49–50, 141
SpaceX, 50
Stallman, Richard, 103
Stationers' Company, 98
Sterling, Bruce, 131
stock markets, 25, 31
Stone, Amasa, 129
Stop Online Piracy Act (SOPA),
  93–94, 151
Stuxnet, 37
sulan, 11, 29, 65
Supreme Court of the United
  States, 120

taxation, 20–21, 88
tax havens, 114
Telecommunications Act (1996),
  107, 132
Teleflex, 120

telephone pirates, 131–132
territoriality, 4–5, 17–28.
  See also sovereignty and
  sovereign states
  boundary creation and, 41–42,
    56–57, 101–102
  cyberspace and, 101–110
  genetic engineering and,
    133–143
  intellectual property rights
    and, 117–121
  maritime, 125
  monopolies and, 95–96
  outer space and, 49–50
  pirate organizations and, 155
  pirate radio and, 83–85
  uncharted areas and, 15
  warfare and, 50–51
Titan Rain campaign, 36–37
too big to fail, 156
trade, international
  agreements on, 61
  capitalist view of, 20
  charters for, 44
  deterritorialization and,
    21–23
  impact of piracy on, 63–64
  monopolies and, 87–99
  normalization of the seas
    and, 26
  pirates versus corsairs and,
    29–39
  property rights and, 19–20
  route to the Indies and, 88–90
Treaty of Westminster (1674), 149
Treaty of Westphalia (1648),
  8, 19
TRIPS agreements, 138

trolls, 7, 116–121, 123, 125
tulip bubble/crisis, 25

UN Convention on the Law of
    the Sea (1982), 67
United Provinces, 26, 60, 89
    corsairs and, 30–32
United States Patent and
    Trademark Office, 118,
    120, 138–139
UNIX, 95

value creation, 42
Van Eyck, Jan, 33
Van Heemskerk, Admiral, 30–32
Venter, Craig, 133, 134–137
Visa, 97

warfare
    pirate organizations and,
        60–61
    radio and, 83–84
    territorial expansion and,
        50–51
Watson, James, 48
Weber, Max, 54
West India Company, 60
Westphalia, Treaty of (1648),
    8, 19
WHN radio station, 91
WikiLeaks, 6, 37, 52, 67, 97,
    143, 146
    goal of, 68–69
Wikipedia, 93–94
World Trade Organization, 138
World Wars, 38, 81, 83–84
Wozniak, Steve, 131

ABOUT THE AUTHORS

Rodolphe Durand is the GDF-Suez Professor of Strategy at HEC Paris where he chairs the Strategy department. Recently, he was Visiting Scholar at Harvard Business School (2012) and Cambridge University, and Visiting Professor at New York University (2011). His work on the social underpinnings of competitive advantage has received international awards including the R. Scott Award (American Sociological Association, 2005) and the European Academy of Management/Imagination Lab Award for Innovative Scholarship (2010).

Jean-Philippe Vergne is a social scientist interested in socially contested organizations. He researches this topic in the context of pirate organizations as well as in today's global arms industry. His work has received several academic distinctions, including the Grigor McClelland Doctoral Dissertation Award. JP is currently a professor of strategy and organization at the Richard Ivey School of Business, Western University (Canada).